D0773512

"If I believed in bishops, I'd want one like Will Willimon—flawed, fearless, and wickedly funny. So I am relieved to say that his memoir in retirement is no more and no less honest than his preaching has been. *Accidental Preacher* reveals a real human being who has been consistent in his commitments to Christ, the church, and the truth, since childhood, but then gives us the quirky backstory on how he came by all that energy and honesty."

— LILLIAN DANIEL, preacher and author of
Tired of Apologizing for a Church I Don't Belong To

"With his exceptional capacity for simple teaching of profound subjects, Will Willimon invites us into his own story, which he reads from the perspective and the experience of faith. An exceptional example of theology at its best—not theology as a discussion of abstract doctrines, but rather theology as the discernment of God's work in human life and history. Highly recommended for preachers of the gospel, but also for any seeking to live the gospel in its fullness."

— JUSTO L. GONZÁLEZ, church historian

"Bishop Will Willimon is a Jesus-loving, story-telling, truth-talking, laugh-generating gift from God for the church. You might think this memoir is about him, but it is really about God, a God who calls, unwittingly, unexpectedly, accidentally. But nothing with God is accidental, not even your reading of this book. So when you open these pages that preach, you'll thank God that you did! This is a literary gem, an honest and holy revelation about vocation."

— LUKE A. POWERY, Duke University Chapel

"It is all here in this compelling memoir: Will Willimon the storyteller, the wit, the sage, the prophet, the pastor, the preacher. But most of all, we encounter Willimon the servant of the church and the unrelenting follower of Christ. This is the story of how, out of the

South, with its monuments already crumbling, and out of a family challenged to its core, comes an eloquent and bold proclaimer of the gospel. As Willimon himself would say, 'Only God and only the church would pull a stunt like that.'"

— Thomas G. Long,
Candler School of Theology

"In this hilarious, moving memoir, Will Willimon both narrates his amazing calling as a preacher and paints a remarkable portrait of the excitement of ordained Christian ministry as a vocation. Take, read, be entertained, and be blessed!"

— L. Gregory Jones, Duke Divinity School

"This is a wonderful book. 'There was things [the author] stretched, but mainly he told the truth.' If Mark Twain had been a Methodist, his name would have been Will Willimon. Will calls his life a 'comedy,' but it's God's own comedy of a southern boy called to preach the truth. Follow the Willimon wit to the source of Willimon's wisdom, and I guarantee you, you won't be disappointed."

— Richard Lischer, author of *Open Secrets*

"Willimon is one of the least obvious persons I have ever known. You might think that his sense of irony means he does not take anything seriously, but then, as this memoir makes clear, Willimon's life is determined by his love of God and, God help him, the Methodist church. The joy and humor at the heart of this memoir not only make it a wonderful read but also indicate how Christians can live well as resident aliens."

— Stanley Hauerwas,
author of *The Character of Virtue*

Accidental Preacher

A Memoir

Will Willimon

With an afterword by Kate Bowler

William B. Eerdmans Publishing Company
Grand Rapids, Michigan

Wm. B. Eerdmans Publishing Co.
4035 Park East Court SE, Grand Rapids, Michigan 49546
www.eerdmans.com

25 24 23 22 21 20 19   1 2 3 4 5 6 7

ISBN 978-0-8028-7644-7

Library of Congress Cataloging-in-Publication Data
Names: Willimon, William H., author.
Title: Accidental preacher : a memoir / Will Willimon ; with an afterword by
    Kate Bowler.
Description: Grand Rapids : Eerdmans Publishing Co., 2019.
Identifiers: LCCN 2019002579 | ISBN 9780802876447 (hardcover : alk. paper)
Subjects: LCSH: Willimon, William H. | United Methodist Church
    (U.S.)—Bishops—Biography. | Preaching.
Classification: LCC BX8495.W6385 A3 2019 | DDC 287/.6092 [B] —dc23
    LC record available at https://lccn.loc.gov/2019002579

Scripture references, unless otherwise noted, are from the King James Version of
the Bible.

Drawings by the author.

Ac·ci·den·tal, ˌaksə'den(t)l, *adjective*: unwitting, fortuitous, inadvertent, unexpected, unplanned, adventitious, serendipitous, unanticipated, unforeseen. Also unlooked-for, unpremeditated, fluky.

Prelude

There was a certain disciple at Damascus, named Ananias; and to him said the Lord in a vision, Ananias . . . Arise, and go into the street which is called Straight, and inquire in the house of Judas for one called Saul. . . . Ananias answered, Lord, I have heard by many of this man, how much evil he hath done. . . . But the Lord said unto him, Go . . . he is a chosen vessel unto me, to bear my name before the Gentiles, and kings, and the children of Israel: For I will shew him how great things he must suffer for my name's sake. (Acts 9:10–16)

Forget the sermons you've heard on Paul's "conversion"—he was already quite happily Jewish—what knocked Paul down on the Damascus road was *vocation*. Saul wasn't searching for a more fulfilling life; he was stalking followers of The Way. The risen Christ confronted Saul the religious terrorist not with promises of a happier life but with an assignment: God's got a job for you, and, by the way, you will suffer because of God's call, forced to worship God with people for whom you had contempt.

In *Surprised by Joy*, C. S. Lewis's account of how God "closed in on me," Lewis mocks "amiable Agnostics" who prattle about humanity's "search for God." That makes as much sense as speaking of "the mouse's search for the cat." God looks for us before we search for God. "You would not have found Me if I had not first found you," said God to Pascal.

My curriculum vitae is a string of incursions when unexpectedly, often belatedly, I discovered that I was being pursued by a God who refuses to take no for an answer.

The God who mugged Church Enemy Number One Saul is the God who refuses to stay dead *and* delights in working up the unlikeliest into "chosen vessels" to bear "my name before the Gentiles, and kings, and the children of Israel." The God who thought it a good idea to have a person like Saul speak up for God could choose anybody.

My story is a comedy, as opposed to a tragedy, not because my life is funny but because my life is having a happy ending due to God's gracious choice to be God for us *and* choosing even the likes of me to be for God. When Rousseau begins his *Confessions*, he brashly boasts that his life is "unlike any other." The claim of this book is just the opposite. I'm betting that you and I both must eventually come to terms with a God who enlists—who shows up at odd times asking, "What have you done for me lately?"—luring us into the happy life we'd have missed if our lives were up to us.

You can tell that Kathleen Norris is a Christian. As she wrote her memoir, she repeatedly reminded herself, "You're not that big of a deal. The call is the big deal." If my memoir makes me my life's chief protagonist, me, the big deal, I'm the most miserable of writers. More interesting than my life are the hijinks of a vocative God who explains my life.

1

Fortuitous Baptism

In the beginning God created the heaven and the earth.
And the earth was without form, and void; and darkness
was upon the face of the deep. And the Spirit of God moved
upon the face of the waters. And God said, Let there be light:
and there was light. And God saw the light, that it was good.
(Genesis 1:1–4)

I never meant to be Methodist. Didn't have to. My forebears allegedly founded octagonal McBee Chapel Methodist Church in the 1830s. (On the back of the second pew to the rear right, you can still see *Roy ROjERs* carved by my brother Bud one Sunday as my mother dozed.) Riding home from church, transfixed by a passing field overcome with kudzu (the one crop that cooperated with the Willimons), I asked, "Am I a Christian?"

Mother answered, "Of course. And Methodist, by virtue of your father's family. You were christened in Mama's living room—after the preacher consumed a fried chicken, three ears of corn, and a peck of okra. Sad man. Vanderbilt Phi Beta Kappa but, because he was a Methodist preacher, none of his five children could afford college." She sighed. "The sacrifices God requires of a preacher's family!" (I had already heard rumors of what God told father Abraham to do to his boy on Mount Moriah, so I was unsurprised by God's rough handling of our preacher.)

"But what if I don't want to be Methodist?" I persisted.

"That will not be possible," she replied.

Luther said baptism is a rite that takes only a few moments to perform but your whole life to complete. The Christian life is spent figuring out what baptism got us into. Though I eventually had theological qualms about the manner of my baptism in my grandmother's living room by a well-educated, underpaid, over-stuffed preacher, it seemed right that one was made Methodist Christian without having say in the matter. Jesus's yoke, desired or not, came with all the other commitments made for, rather than by, you. Zwingli compared baptismal naming to the bestowal of

a monk's cowl. The clothing of a monk came in one size. When a boy joined a monastery, he received a cowl fit for a man. The child probably looked ridiculous wearing a grown man's robe. Yet with time, the young monk grew to the cowl until one day it fit.

So with baptism, the name "Christian" is superimposed on our family name. It's absurd to call a little baby, squalling in his grandmother's living room after Sunday dinner, "Christian." Yet that's just what the church does until, sooner or later, the promises of baptism are fulfilled; we have become that person who the church promised we would be. Somebody calls out, "Christian," and we answer because, by the grace of God, the name fits.

As the implications of my baptism unfolded, I discovered what Barbara Brown Taylor said of the descending Holy Spirit in Jesus's baptism—"This dove has got a set of claws."

*   *   *

But enough about God; back to me.

Rosy-fingered dawn lights the window, revealing a boy abed on a warm May morning three days before his eighth birthday. The night chorus of crickets is silent. A thrush, a robin, and maybe a wren sing to the breeze that sways the surrounding pines. A distant tractor—by the sound, Uncle Charles's John Deere diesel—works the field behind the woods. From the kitchen, a pan clangs as Mother makes breakfast—grits, inevitably.

The pine-paneled bedroom had been passed to me by my much older brother Bud when he escaped Greenville for the navy. This, my world—the room encrusted with curiosities from fields and woods, the rock house in the middle of a pine forest in the Carolina Piedmont, nearest neighbors a quarter mile down Fork Shoals Road—alone, but for my mother.

She had designed the house on two sheets of paper. As she said, "Furman Carr and a colored man named James" built the house before I was born, using posts and planks cut at the family sawmill, with the house veneered in reddish fieldstone salvaged from the chimneys of abandoned tenant houses that were once homes for the twenty families who worked my grandfather's cotton farm.

By the time I arrived the sharecroppers had bolted. The once thriving "Willimon Place" was two thousand acres of memory in red clay. The dozen barns were bare, the fields were briars and bitter weed, though the forsaken Willimon Cotton Gin was well used, perfect for Saturday enactments of *The Lone Ranger.* Each irregular red rock that covered the house where I awakened came from a little world where nobody moved in and few left, even the dead.

In Scripture, God knows everybody's name. Sometimes when God calls, God changes their names; Saul famously became Paul, Abram shifted to Abraham, Sarai to Sarah. The disciples are just so-and-so's son until Jesus puts the finger on them, and thereafter they are Andrew or Peter, suggesting that theologian Karl Barth is right: one is not a full person until one is addressed.

I awoke to my name—Willy or sometimes Billy in my first decade—in the pine-paneled room in the rock house in the middle of a cluster of pines. Mother preferred William, because I was named for my grandfather, the recently departed, well-admired patriarch William Henry Willimon, who *South Carolina Families* claimed was "benevolent to all his hands, colored and white."

"Papa," William Henry Willimon, had been named for his father, William Henry Abraham Willimon, who graduated from the University of Kentucky with a diploma in "Railroading, Boiler

Making, Accounting, Animal Husbandry, Business, Law, and Rhetoric."

When he returned from the Civil War, W. H. A. Willimon slept on the floor rather than a bed for the rest of his days as atonement for the South's loss. When my mother died, I was given the chest where William Henry Abraham Willimon kept his Confederate uniform, though by that time his prized gray outfit was dust. All that was known of family prehistory was "our people came to the upcountry from down near Charleston." Beyond that, history was silent until Jacob and Esau, Cain and Abel, Adam and Eve.

On the first day of fifth grade my strange-but-occasionally-nice teacher signaled that "William" was unsatisfactory. She much preferred Will—"Dr. Will Fewell spent his life curbing drunkenness in Greenville. Will Rogers was a wonderful man. Died in the crash of Wiley Post's plane. You shall be Will."

It stuck. Thus I learned you couldn't choose who you wanted to be. God called the light good, then named Adam and Eve. One night, Abram got renamed Abraham and couldn't do anything about it. In Bethlehem, Jesus was prenatally named by an angel. Saul became Paul. In Greenville, an old maid schoolteacher—who taught that Franklin Roosevelt had a bossy wife, and Harry Truman was Missouri white trash—named you. Names were accidents, additions that make you, you—Will, Sandlapper, Democrat, Methodist. Names are bestowed or imposed, gifted or coerced, depending on how you look at it.

*   *   *

Christians are obsessed with history not only because that's where God incarnates but also because, as Moses discovered (Exod. 33:20–23), God is most safely and accurately viewed through a rearview mirror. James Baldwin, in "The Price of the Ticket," said that you must do history: go back to where you began, tell the truth about it, and then do it over. We have more future with God than past, Kierkegaard said, and though life must be lived forward, life is only understood backward, making historians of us all.

The American South has produced more history than it has been able to consume. Most of life that was handed me was in the past tense—ruins of tenant houses; the deserted black church surrounded by a ruined cemetery; six threatening, dark, dangerous abandoned wells; two fishing ponds; a dozen empty barns; a handful of Confederate Reunion medals. My people savored the past, chewed it, and regurgitated it to nourish the nestlings.

Why had no one filled those menacing wells? One uncle explained, "To teach boys to watch where they're going. My boy, experience, you will find, is a most vauable teacha. If hit don't kill you."

*   *   *

For an imaginative boy, rusting farm machinery, cleared of honeysuckle and kudzu, became a bomber for thirty seconds over Tokyo. If you taunted death by climbing the creaking stairs, then clambered up the ladder to the topmost of the big barn, you could push back the rusted tin and see all the way to Greenville, even to the Blue Ridge beyond. My mother claimed that the cotton gin was once "the center of economic life in this part of the county." By the time I got there, it was Camelot.

Harry Crews opens his autobiography, *A Childhood*, with this: "Nothing is allowed to die in a society of storytelling people." Perhaps an inchoate desire for immortality, a sense that they were a dying breed, made Willimons virtuoso storytellers.

During one Sunday dinner somebody in law enforcement was labeled a "Neanderthal Baptist from Pendleton."

"Pendleton is pathologically archaic," chimed an uncle.

"So backward," discoursed Uncle Henry, "that when Jesus returns the only place he'll recognize is Pendleton." Guffaws of agreement around the table.

"That's ridiculous," countered Uncle Gene (who once took a football thirty yards down the Clemson field in the wrong direction before being tackled by his own team). "America wasn't discovered until 1492. Pendleton wasn't even here when Jesus was."

When a cousin left for Clemson, thus opening a space at the table, I joined in the dinner talk. I was formally initiated by an uncle: "One day Papa—you're his namesake, Willie—came home from the office and put on a pair of overalls and began rakin' the front yard. A man ambled down Fork Shoals, stopped, leaned against the fence, and tried to be sociable.

"'Mighty hot day to be out working,' the man said to Papa. Papa just nodded and kept rakin'. Unlike Mama, Papa didn't take much to talking with people he didn't know.

"'Can't believe that rakin's worth doin' in this heat,' said the man.

"'Still got to be done,' said Papa, aggravated.

"'Yep, I always heard these Willimons was sons-a-bitches to work for,' said the man.

"Papa run that man way down the road with his rake." Gales of laughter.

Stories helped us make sense and mount a defense. In my formative years, Grandmother's Sunday dinner table was a stage for elaborate public narration of the past. When the bucket was let down for life-giving refreshment, stories were all the family had to pull up—long, involved tales of prosperity before Sherman's troops came through "like an army of ravening locusts, I tell you," and stole or burned everything "they couldn't cart off." Legends of outlandish moments in the lives of uncles and aunts on visits to Chicago or Charleston; memorable last plays in Clemson football; dark, whispered shenanigans of trash who lived down the road and were rumored to be Republicans; and testimonials to loyal "Negroes" who, in times of trouble, showed more smarts than "most white people." Stories kept the family going as the Hebrews were given manna in the wilderness. Adults didn't spend much time thinking about what's next; in their stories, tomorrow would never match yesterday.

Years later an ingrate reviewed my big book on Barth, saying, "Willimon rambles; still, the ramblings are the best of his book."

Some afternoons with my dog, I visited the foundations of my great-grandfather's house, the very spot where my heroic great-grandmother buried the silverware when the Yankees came through laying waste a perfect world. "Do you have a mother?" she reputedly asked one of the Yankees as family treasures were looted. "How the poor woman must grieve that she bore the likes of you!"

I walked off the lines of the foundation, baffled that the manor (*"one of the grandest houses in Greenville County"*) was smaller than I had been led to believe.

Each afternoon I shuffled from the school bus stop—where Ashmore Bridge Road meets Fork Shoals at the old gin—to my grandmother's house. (I rode the yellow bus for an hour each way, never questioning why we passed by three "colored schools.") At Mama's, a quarter of a mile down Fork Shoals, I sat enthralled by her stories as I awaited Mother coming home after her day of teaching at Greenville High.

Our home was a matriarchy. Each weekday ended with my mother, after clearing the dishes, setting up shop on our dining room table, grading papers or working on the next day's lesson into the night. After my mother's death, I received condolences from her supervisor at the state board of education: "Never did your mother enter her classroom unprepared. Her lesson plans were a mixture of creativity and realism, wonderfully focused. She cared for each of her students, but never more than she cared for the inculcation of the subject." The night before her funeral, a grief-stricken, unknown woman came through our receiving line wailing, "Your mother taught me how to do a cheese soufflé that doesn't fall!"

I've not had a day as physically and intellectually demanding as my mother's average day at Greenville High. When one of my readers complained that I overloaded my writing with words nobody uses, I explained, "Winn-Dixie gave away coupons with groceries. One year a hundred coupons won your choice of an un-abridged Webster's dictionary or a set of ice-tea glasses. Proudly my mother lugged home a five-pound Webster's, the only person in Greenville to take the dictionary rather than the glasses."

My grandmother, "Mama," though crippled with arthritis, he-roically tried to supervise the farming of eleven hundred acres. Even as my grandfather had ridden a white horse each evening to inspect the crops, she drove her black Plymouth at 5 p.m. to oversee the cotton, sometimes sending me out from the car to direct the hands for the next day's work or having me collect a couple of bolls for her close inspection.

Women ruled, even when men were present. Any uncle tossing his napkin aside for emphasis and making a loud, *ex tabula* pro-nouncement at Sunday dinner invariably sought validation from a nearby aunt, "Isn't that right, honey?" An aunt would murmur ma-ternally, "Yes, dear, it's the gospel truth," while he basked boyishly.

Mama's sprawling home welcomed with a large, embracing front porch that wrapped around two sides of the house, perfect for hot afternoons and a genteel wave to passersby. Of course, the front porch welcome was reserved for white visitors; any person of color, no matter how highly valued by the family, was con-signed to stand hat-in-hand at the back door as Mama demon-strated her gentility by offering a cool drink from a jelly jar.

A room on the front of Mama's housed a succession of new-lyweds who began married life under supervision. Occasionally visiting relatives occupied the newlywed room. Some second cousin showed up from out of state. After dinner he made a nest in the newlywed room, where he unapologetically squatted for weeks. One Sunday dinner, into the second month of the cousin's stay, Uncle Henry jovially said to the cousin-in-residence (hoping he would take a hint), "We wouldn't want to take advantage of your sociability so as to interfere with your commercial responsibilities. Don't feel you need to linger here at Mama's just because we relish the pleasure of your company, har, har, har."

As he helped himself to more collards, the cousin reassured Henry that he had no intention of leaving anytime soon. The cousin boarded two more years.

Willimons bragged of past prosperity. Mama's house boasted the first plastered ceilings in that part of the county. Around the Sunday dinner table, where serious, sustained recollection occurred, they said that, before the war, on Sunday afternoons passersby would stop, knock, and ask if they could see the wonder.

"You ain't afraid to sleep under that at night?" strangers said, gaping. Everyone around the table snickered at the simplicity of the common folk.

By the time I took my place in family photos, Willimons were "land poor," rich only in stories. The family confirmed their superiority to white trash renters by referring to "our Neeegroes" rather than by more common designations. Notably, I had no friend of my own race until I was seven.

If life on "the place" was so good before my birth, and folks— black and white—lived then in harmony, why did all the Negroes move north first chance they got? What's Detroit that Greenville isn't?

*   *   *

Flannery O'Connor declared that "people from the North are not from anywhere." No tourist just passing through, I for good or ill was located. Years later, as *Gastprofessor* in Bonn, at a faculty wine and cheese party, the *Dekan* asked, "Herr Professor Willimon, welches Thema der Theologie verfolgen Sie, während Sie in Deutschland sind?" (What subject are you pursuing in Germany?)

"I'm a homiletician; Germany is the last place anybody would study practical theology. I'm here because I'm from South Carolina. We engaged in a vast social evil. Germany committed evil. We got caught. You got caught. Though your repentance is more sincere than ours." It was the dean's last question.

Formal political instruction came by overhearing uncles' arguments during protracted Sunday dinners at Mama's house. The opening blessing rarely occurred before two-thirty, and the table was not cleared until nearly dusk.

"Some of the ignorantest people come from Edgefield, I tell you, Willie, and not only the Baptists," Uncle Charles pronounced in response to a request for a ruling on Edgefield-bred senator J. Strom Thurmond.

"That's the gospel truth," agreed Uncle Gene in a rare affirmation of another uncle's adjudication.

"Thieving, low-country politicians out of Barnwell ruined this state," added Uncle Henry, moving wider the geographical bounds of political ineptitude. That Henry was a lawyer and had married a Jewish woman whose family owned Greenville's biggest department store added clout to his pronouncements.

An oft-repeated political parable was of the Greenville Christmas parade when Governor Thurmond showed off by riding a huge white horse down Main Street in front of the Shriners.

Pointing to him, my cousin Rusty asked, "Who's that?"

"Don't you know?" exclaimed Uncle Gene. "That's J. Strom Thurmond."

Rusty persisted: "Who's that old man on top of J. Strom Thurmond?"

They rarely told you anything worth knowing face-to-face. Really important truth was overheard, some of the most truthful never spoken. When I was a year old, a mob of Greenville whites dragged black Willie Earle from his jail cell in Pickens and tortured him to death out near the Greenville Pickens Speedway (one of the many businesses that my father owned and lost). The lynching and subsequent trial (in which the confessed lynchers were acquitted by the all-white Greenville jury) were the biggest thing that ever happened in Greenville, attracting attention from all over the world.

Odd, they forgot to mention the lynching. So, later I had to carve out a couple of years for research and wrote *Who Lynched Willie Earle?* to make up for Greenville's conspiracy of silence.

During a major political debate one Sunday at table, I ventured, "Are we going to vote for General Eisenhower?" Stunned, awkward dismay all round.

Mama maternally patted my hand. "No, dear. He is a Republican. We are Democrats." Murmurs of agreement in the assembly.

"Never met anybody with any sense in the army," added one of the uncles, "'specially the generals. Please pass the chicken. Government leeches." Consumption resumed.

"Are there Republicans around here?" I persisted.

Aggravated silence.

Mama adjusted the napkin in her lap and patiently responded, "No, dear, not that we know of."

"Well, where are Republicans?" I continued. (I had seen pictures of them on stamps in my album.)

An uncle dropped his fork clanging into his plate and threw up his hands. "Good Lord, God A'mighty."

"They tend to live in Illinois and Michigan, places of that nature." She sighed patiently.

"Why are they Republicans and we are Democrats?"

Those at table believed Mama had been overly indulgent. "Child, if people live by choice in places like Illinois and Michigan, they will be strange in other ways too."

"Amen," said somebody.

In college, I participated in a 1966 statewide student debate on the war in Vietnam. In response to my presentation the dean of students at the University of South Carolina (retired army colonel) stamped and snorted, "You leftist students are ruining this country. It's unthinkable that America would lose a war!"

Recalling the mythmaking evasion of my white Southern family, I quipped, "Sure you can. I've got uncles who could teach you how."

First time I ran for bishop (without appearing to be running for bishop; no small feat), I withdrew from the balloting. An officious layperson bustled up and said haughtily, "Reverend Willimon, I was offended by your concession speech."

"Offended?" I responded. "I withdrew! You should be pleased. I lost."

"You sounded arrogant, like you thought you were the only person who could change the Methodist church."

"How could I be both a loser and arrogant?" I asked.

A layperson from Mississippi, standing nearby explained, "Will's from South Carolina. Hell, his people have been both defeated and arrogant for two hundred years!"

In the *Analects*, Confucius advises, "Respect ghosts and spirits, but keep them at a distance." This is great wisdom I've never obeyed.

*   *   *

Back then, few strutted around bragging about their astute exercise of choice. Life's most formative events happened to you before you could do much about them. "It's just God's will" never explained anything good; there was acceptance of (or resignation to?) life's inevitabilities. Resistance was futile. Make the best of whatever Providence dumps upon you, tighten your belt, buckle down, and hold your head high as you play the hand you were dealt. God doesn't like whiners.

A chief aspect of my comedy: *I was born incapable of disbelief.* Maybe it came with baptism. Or was innate credulousness a byproduct of birth in South Carolina? South Carolinians believed it sensible to send Strom Thurmond to the Senate, perennially, even though the uncles around the Sunday dinner table agreed that "poor old Strom" was in his dotage—"bless his heart"—had fathered a black child—"I hear tell"—and was Washington's most active "skirt chaser"—"I am reliably informed by a girl that works at the post office." Anybody who thought that Democrat-turned-Dixiecrat-turned-Republican Strom was God's gift to South Carolina found believing that Jesus walked on water or took out a herd of swine easy.

Postbaptismal instruction occurred every morning with Bible stories at breakfast, read by Mother from *Hurlbut's*, the masterwork of a New York Methodist who pounded Israel's stories into generations of unsuspecting children. Flannery O'Connor said that while the South was no longer the Bible Belt, it was still "Christ-haunted" because it was peopled by "the descendants of old ladies" who "read the Bible on their knees." My mother ended her day reading her bedside Bible. That one so fiercely independent as my mother daily submitted to the writings of these ancient Jews made a deep impression.

Church, as far as I could tell, was where you overheard talk with God, though the church's talk about God was less interesting than *Hurlbut's* stories of God. The preacher talked to God in prayers, and God talked back to the preacher, who, in sermons, let you in on what he had heard. There was a repeated hint, in sermons, that God had done some mean-spirited things in Bible times and might pull similar stunts again, if Jehovah had a mind to. Pray that America cured the current outbreak of juvenile delinquency instigated by James Dean and Elvis, found a way to blow up Castro before he took Miami, and that the Lord kept his eyes on that rainbow.

Everybody knew there was a God, though there was a division over whether or not God bore a grudge against South Carolina. The decline of cotton prices, boll weevils, as well as the stupidity of Republicans in Congress suggested limits on divine goodness. If God sat back and allowed the South to lose the war, how else might God fail to live up to expectations?

Not until my early twenties, at Yale Divinity School, did I meet an honest-to-God unbeliever, an aspiring atheist from Minnesota. For me, a South Carolinian, my baptism by God was indelible; whether or not God was good remained an open question.

One night at a student party in Hopkins House at Yale, I, a first-year seminarian under the influence, told (accompanied by copious hand gestures) a perfectly wonderful story from my days at Greenville High. In response, Midwestern Atheist Wannabe whined, nasally, "Is that really true?"

In all my years as a renowned frat-party fabulist, never had I encountered such ingratitude, such disrespect for creativity. My heart went out to the poor dolt. Closing my eyes, I knelt and prayed, *Lord, I believe, enlarge my credulity.*

*   *   *

As a teenager, I once asked my mother to confirm that we had never been slave owners. She arose, went to the bureau, and pulled out a photocopy of an ancient receipt. "For the sum of one hundred dollars, a negro male, of about twenty years of age." Signed, "William Henry Abraham Willimon." She put the receipt back in the drawer for such time as it was required for further moral instruction.

Though hailing from South Carolina is not my fault, the land of my nativity has imbued me with enough candor to admit to some of my sin. The original, innate sin of South Carolinians is so pervasive that we are not free to consider the possibility of either our innocence or of the nonexistence of a forgiving God. It's our only hope.

Sometime after midnight in the summer of '65, Amsterdam, a group of us expats were lounging in the Dam Square, unanimous on the stupidity of the Vietnam War, taking turns singing, "I'm a more committed bomb-throwing radical than you," to the guitar accompaniment of a frizzled Californian straight from *Hair*. Suddenly, a student from Berlin—with whom I had tried to have a conversation using my Wofford German—lunged, grabbed my throat, and yelled in slurred, drunken fury, "Du Gott verdammte unschuldige, reine, verdammte Amerikaner . . ." (You God-damned innocent Americans! I'm glad you got caught. Vietnam is your day of judgment. Burning babies. Napalm. You won the "good war," so you think you can tell us what to do. Now, you're no better than us.)

"Dein Großvater hat meine Großmutter vergewaltigt als die amerikanische Armee meine Stadt übernahm. Das haben sie dir nicht erzählt, oder?" (Your grandfather raped my grandmother when the American army took my town. They forgot to tell you about that, did they?)

"Unschuldige Amerikaner."

As he spit and sputtered away, cursing us innocents abroad, from a safe distance I shouted, "I'm from South Carolina! Like I need some damn German to tell me my people have been bad?"

*   *   *

C. S. Lewis claimed that from age six to eight he lived "almost entirely in my imagination." Provoked by the mysteries of the woods and creeks surrounding the field-rock house in the middle of the pines, I did the same.

On an autumn night, the pines hissed eerily, things bumped in the dark, an anonymous cry or the portentous crack of a limb sounded from the woods. On fall mornings, fog crept away from the house and crouched in the creek until dark, physical proof that the pastures and woods were enchanted. Ghosts were real; what you could see, smell, and touch wasn't the half of it. There was no way to avoid being a high sacramentalist, born knowing that the material conveyed the spiritual. Through any of it, God could speak.

My world, though small, was possessed. The dead refused to stay that way, appearing not only in stories by uncles. I discovered an almost perfect arrowhead unearthed after a rain, not a hundred feet from my rock home. As I turned the wonder in my fingers, I trembled. Then I carefully displayed the arrowhead in my room as confirmation that the woods had been someone else's before they were ours. Like the Israelites in Canaan, we were just passing through. Had the aborigines plans to take back what once was theirs? Things were less stable than I had been taught to believe. The *ancien régime* Willimons, for all their pretensions of immortality, were resident aliens. No way to avoid silent, accusing ghosts.

On nights when I took the dreaded walk to the house down the curving drive that led from Fork Shoals Road—say, when Lewis Haselwood's father brought me home from a Scout meeting in town—moonlight through the pines or a rustle in the surrounding forest, the crickets' chorus, or bullfrogs outshouting one another over who owned the pond were terrifying, but once the porch light finally lit my way to safety, I never let on that I had been afraid.

By day, nature smiled, though sometimes spirits came out in broad daylight; a tree or toad, a ripple on the pond hinted there was more. Once, when I set out for the woods, the old gate into the pasture swung open before me, on its own. There was little wind that day, not enough to explain it. As it opened, the gate said something. I turned heel, ran back to the house, and locked the front door.

When I was in the mood to head toward enchantment rather than run, I roamed the woods. My mother taught school twelve months a year. After my eighth birthday, summer days

from morning to late afternoon were solitary, but never alone. Imagination made good company. From mid-May until the end of August I wore no shirt or shoes (except for church). Free of peering adults, I was led by a host of imaginary companions, as they pleased. Encouraged by my mother, my fancy was stoked by books—*Greek Myths, King Arthur and His Round Table, Tom Sawyer*—and TV shows of the fifties, like *Sergeant Preston of the Yukon*, with his dog, Yukon King. It was an age when it made perfect sense for a kid in Ohio to jump off a roof as Superman and for a boy like me in Virginia to down a spoonful of Red Devil Lye, seeing the skull and crossbones, assuming, of course, that he was eating pirate food. Bliss it was to be a boy in such a time.

Those golden afternoons, the world wasn't inert Nature; it was Creation, alive, thick with meaning. Darting from tree to tree—my Birnam Wood or Forest of Arden, realm of Oberon and Titania (thanks, *Lamb's Tales of Shakespeare*)—saying aloud each of the parts in the play that was in my head. The Lone Ranger in the morning, King Arthur by afternoon, Gene Autry or Sky King before dark. I could wield a sword or swing a battle-ax with the best. As I was calling for help from my unseen-to-all sidekicks, with Robert Peary at the Pole, or doing as I was told by Wyatt Earp in the O.K. Corral, anyone witnessing my dashing about— encouraging comrades, shouting defiance at enemies across the pasture—would have thought me crazy. Solitude has benefits.

My uncle Charles gave me a quarter horse, Peppermint, as if my imagination needed help. Peppermint was only half tamed and loved nothing better than to peel me off her back by darting under a low hanging branch as she galloped back to the barn. Yet even obstinate Peppermint was Trigger or Silver in the mind of a kid who knows he's Sky King.

My fifth summer, Mother took a children's literature course at Peabody. When she came home and read aloud *Winnie the Pooh*, I collapsed into laughter and demanded to have it read again, then please, just one more time. "That's when I knew I had a child who was obsessed with words," she recalled.

"When I was one, I had just begun. . . . Now that I'm six, I'm as clever as clever. I think I'll stay six for ever and ever." My house was Pooh Corner in the middle of the Hundred Acre Wood.

Crabby Malcolm Muggeridge sniggered, "No child ever liked Winnie the Pooh except to ingratiate themselves to adults." Perhaps my affection for Milne's Pooh proves I was more adult than child.

Pauline—the black woman who kept me during the day— read to me every afternoon. Sitting in her lap as she uncovered the wonders in the books was my day's highlight. She pointed to the details in the pictures and took on different voices for each of the characters. Why were the books read by Pauline so much more interesting than the same books read by my mother each evening? I became angry when Mother failed to read the story as it was. She laughed and pointed to the words on the page.

Later, I learned that Pauline couldn't read.

✳   ✳   ✳

During some primal storm a huge tree at the woods' edge had fallen. About twenty feet up its downed trunk, the poplar had put forth two huge branches and kept growing upward. What determination!

"I've knelt down for you," the healing tree (Rev. 22:2) once said to me, casually. "Climb along my back. Hoist up my branches, make me a pirate ship or my soft wood a target for your hatchet, my limbs a fort to fight Apaches, secrets between the two of us. It's high time for you to become a boy." I took the tree up on its offer.

Other trees stubbornly refused conquering. Just when you thought you had a good toehold, a limb cracked and you tumbled, defeated by the tree you thought you were subduing. I would stare up, my breath knocked out, the tree looking down at me, gloating.

You had to respect a tree for that.

One day I pulled up a rock in the creek that bubbled out of a spring and fed into the fishing pond in the pasture. A slimy salamander slithered under another rock. "Some of us like our dark better than your light," it whispered upon escape. "There's a world down here, hidden, dark, where you aren't welcome."

That very afternoon, I walked in the house and overheard my mother standing in the hall at the telephone, as people did back then. "Slit his throat with his razor? Bled to death in his front yard? Choked in his own blood, you say? How sad. . . . He was always so helpful at the garage. His last words? 'Mama, I'm thirsty.'"

The salamander was right.

"Who died?" I asked that night at supper.

"None of your concern," I was told. "You should not eavesdrop on private conversations."

How would I find out anything without listening in? And what else are they hiding?

Upon a dare, I slid on my stomach to the rim of an abandoned, dry well and peered down. At the bottom lay the rotting carcass of a dog.

"Dumped there by somebody too lazy to dig a grave," speculated my friend.

"No, he's out sniffing a rabbit and falls in, dead of a broke neck or just starved to death," said I. "I bet there's a story behind it."

Even bad luck can be improved by a good storyteller.

"Hellofaway to go," said my philosophical black friend. "One day you're chasing a rabbit, having one hell of a time, next day, you're by yourself, neck broke at the bottom of a well. I bet he didn't see that coming."

One thing was sure: The world isn't obvious. All awaits discovery. How can the woods be both dry, threatening *Erēmos*, and lush, inviting *Paradeisos*? Who knows what the hoot owl is up to while we sleep? What's the good of slithering salamanders? Was there anybody who missed the dog at the bottom of the well? After supper, did they call the dog's name until they were hoarse? Did anybody go out, like Jesus, and beat the bushes looking for him until dark? The Shepherd searched, found, and brought home the one lost sheep. Was there no one willing to go out into the wilderness to seek a speckled hound?

Thirty years later when I read Karl Barth declare that God could speak through Russian communism, a flute concerto, a

Mozart sonata, or a dead dog, I muttered, *Tell me something I don't know.*

The mystery and embrace of my world make strange the compulsion to leave the Willimon place, once I got the chance. Why weren't the woods, the pond, the abandoned wells, the uncles, and the crickets enough? Adam and Eve were kicked out of Eden by God; I packed up and left on my own, venturing as far as Wofford College, thirty miles away.

Or did I? Abraham had to wait until he was old ("and him as good as dead," said Paul, Heb. 11:12) before God told him to leave the land he knew and venture where he knew not. The disciples were grown-ups when Jesus invited them to abandon their families and the fishing and hit the road. When I climbed the ladder and pushed open the sheet of tin on top of the barn so that I could see as far as Greenville, what mysteriousness beckoned beyond the Blue Ridge? Though the Willimons' land was no prison, something made me think, *These two thousand haunted acres are not enough. God Almighty is not limited, even to this.*

While Boswell's Dr. Johnson said that "to be happy at home" is the supreme end of human endeavor, my mother thought otherwise. She placed a huge map next to my bed. I stared at it, memorized every country and capital without trying. Printed before World War II, the map was mostly pink, to indicate what Kipling claimed to be British. My two albums full of world stamps infected me with a yearning to visit the places on the stamps, the lands of the map. In *Nobody Knows My Name* James Baldwin explained why "the American writer keeps running off to Europe." No writer can tell the truth of America who does not, in some sense, leave. America distrusts artists, writers, and intellectuals, said Baldwin, because they have had the guts to abandon home. Still, abandoning home is the only way to find it.

Or maybe it was God. In olden days God was always ordering people to go to this land or that, to take it by force if they had to. When some of the Israelites were content to stay slaves in Egypt, Yahweh was infuriated by their resistance to relocation. In a fit of anger God almost wiped out the Hebrews when they cowered like grasshoppers on the threshold of the promised land (Num. 13–14). Saint Paul, according to the plywood map of his missionary journeys that hung in the youth Sunday school room at Buncombe Street Methodist, stayed nowhere long. Jesus, as everybody knows, traveled to excess, boasting of nowhere to lay his head.

I'm sure that one of the many reasons I eventually fell in love with an itinerating Methodist preacher's daughter was that her childhood, unlike mine, was a series of forced relocations. True, Patsy's childhood moves were from Little River, to Cheraw, to Dillon, to (thank God) Greenville at the behest of a bishop. As I've explored Stockholm, St. Petersburg, Singapore, or Seoul after giving a sermon or lecture, I've thought, *I'm the last of a dying breed—the truly itinerant Methodist preacher.*

"Will Willimon is like the Holy Spirit—here, there, everywhere—except in church," quipped a smart-aleck bishop.

Mother was brought south by her failure-at-farming father, who packed up his dairy cows and came all the way from exotic Maxbass, North Dakota. Rumor has it that "Papa," the grandfather I hardly knew, left North Dakota because he never forgave God for the death of my mother's mother. (Mama Willimon, according to the recollection of the uncles, "never forgave God for the death of baby Francis.") No wonder Jesus commanded, "Love your enemies" (Matt. 5:44).

One of my mother's few memories of North Dakota was being lifted up to an open casket to kiss her Quaker mother whose body was packed in ice. Though a virtual orphan throughout childhood, she never complained. "You can endure anything except a rock in your shoe," she claimed. Stoicism suited her more than Methodism. Mother's favorite passage? Philippians 4:11—"I have learned, in whatsoever state I am, therewith to be content."

When my sister was twelve (so the story went—I was not born yet), matriarch Mama (as we called my paternal grandmother) took Harriet ("Harry," I called her as soon as I could talk) for an all-day pilgrimage to the state capital in Columbia. Upon her return, Harry threw herself upon our sofa, sobbing.

"What's wrong?" Mother asked. "What happened in Columbia?"

With trembling lips Harry told all: "Mama took me to the capital building. She pointed to bronze stars and showed me the scars in the stone that were caused by General Sherman's cannonballs. Mama said, 'See what your mother's people did to our statehouse!'"

Aggravated Mother replied, "Please inform your grandmother that North Dakota wasn't even a state during the Civil War!"

Did my mother feel at home in the house that she had planned and built in the middle of land that the Willimons claimed as eternally theirs? Mama Willimon became the mother she never had, and the Willimons gave her a place at last to call home. When somebody bragged at having a family in South Carolina that went back generations, my mother dismissively noted that "everybody here is from elsewhere. And what aristocratic family, pray tell, ensconced in an English castle would have ventured a three-month ocean voyage?"

So, why did my mother stay after my father had left? As Naomi's people had become Ruth's, so his people became hers. She was closer to my grandmother than my grandmother's own. Proof: My aunt Ann, competing for Queen of the Rhododendron in faraway Asheville, caused a scandal by having been seen in prolonged conversation with a black man the evening after the pageant. My mother was hurriedly dispatched by the family to retrieve Ann and bring her back to Greenville.

And when my mother died at Duke, after supposedly minor surgery to repair a problem incurred decades earlier in giving birth to me, Uncle Charles called on behalf of the Willimons and offered the last remaining space in the Willimon plot in Springwood Cemetery. Mother lies next to my father's parents, Papa and Mama.

Perhaps her encouraging her children to travel, to go off brashly to see things for themselves, was Mother's escape.

"That's nuts!" a censorious friend said of my mother's permitting me, a high school junior, to spend a summer camping through the West with a couple of college guys, one of whom had a brand-new Chevy Impala. "No responsible parent would allow a sixteen-year-old to do that."

"You don't know my mother," said I.

The travel writer Paul Theroux says that we travel to discover who we really are; the discovery we make in our journeys from home is ourselves, differentiated from our origins. The purpose of Christian travel, contra Theroux, is not self-discovery—you can stay home and do that—but divine assignment.

If you hope to keep up with a living God, be ready to relocate. The God who sent Sarah and Abraham, Jacob, Saul-become-Paul,

Mary, Joseph, and Jesus on fateful journeys gains easier access to people who are far from the safety of home. As chaplain at Duke, I learned that the best way to instigate an encounter with Jesus was to entice students to sign up for a spring mission trip to Honduras or Haiti. When they were stripped of their defenses, on unfamiliar terrain, sleeping on a dirt floor, dependent upon Christians who speak another language, Jesus ambushed them, similar to the way he eventually accosted me.

Harry, my sister, was the first in the family to leave voluntarily, venturing all the way to William and Mary when I was two, absconding to Virginia. Her college years provided the most exotic adventures of my early life. I bunked in the Tri-Delt sorority house where the girls shouted, "Man on the hall," as I entered. I rode in the bellhop's bicycle basket when we stayed at the Williamsburg Inn and fired a colonial musket at the Powder Magazine. Harry was a drama major (the department's first Phi Beta Kappa), went to big dances in Richmond, and played Martha Washington in Williamsburg's outdoor pageant, "The Common Glory."

When Harry came home from school, I got to stay up until midnight and go to the depot to witness the earthshaking arrival of the Southerner as it roared and clanged into Greenville. Then I would sit on her bed as she unpacked, laid out magic potions on her dresser, and told tales of never-never land called college. Her college boyfriend George sent me a Jackie Robinson doll in uniform with a little bat, surely hoping to distract the little brother while he courted my big sister.

More worlds lay beyond the Blue Ridge that bordered Greenville, wonders elsewhere. With the things of God, there's always more. When for the first time a high school biology teacher invited me to peer through a microscope, my suspicions were confirmed. Other students gaped in wonder, but I merely smiled, whispering, *I knew there was more*. Tiny beings in motion, changing shape, with a dozen feet rushing somewhere, sent on errands God only knows, busy. Hardly anything is solid. Nothing is still. All, summoned, hide and seek, teasing somebody to decode their purpose. Everything, even paramecia, called toward something rather than nothing, making their own way in the world. And what about me? When will God take me somewhere dangerous?

*   *   *

Thank God I got to be a lonely child in a world that gave me vast stretches of time unsupervised, unmonitored by adults and free of the stress and censure that come from overexposure to peers. God abhors a vacuum, loves to intrude into empty spaces, likes nothing better than to disrupt solitude. Surely that's why Judaism, Christianity, and Islam arose in an arid, deserted corner of the world with few trees to hide behind. "I sat alone because of thy hand," said the prophet (Jer. 15:17).

Granted, the world around me was not a knockdown argument for God—nothing in the world can be that—but it prodded me to expect more. As Thoreau said, some evidence, though circumstantial, is irrefutable, as when one finds a trout in a pail of milk. If the world in which I had been deposited was a gift, surely there was a Giver.

Sunday school—where they dressed you in wool trousers to hear stories about Jesus—was somewhat helpful in decoding the world. Mr. Sanders—superintendent of the primary division at Buncombe Street Methodist Church—paid quarters for Scripture memorization. I got my quarter for memorizing John 3:16, "God so loved the world, that he gave his only begotten Son, that whosoever believeth in him should not perish, but have everlasting life."

As an easy believer, I already knew I was a certified "whosoever." But I needed the Bible to tell me *God so loved*. Nature can't preach, can't disclose the Trinity, even to one so attuned as my friend Wendell Berry. William Carlos Williams was right, "We cannot go to the country . . . the country will bring us no peace." That the world has been, is being loved is a truth that must be revealed, a truth inaccessible through walks in the woods. Pantheism is trifling evasion of the difficulty of having God show up as a Jew from Nazareth.

John 3:16 meant that the world in which I roam, the wide woods once fearsome, sometimes delightful, the trees, the pasture, the abandoned wells and the rocks that surround my house are here for no better telos than love. The world—the magic poplar, the grief for the gas station owner who slit his throat and bled to death in his front yard, the slithering salamander, Mr. Sanders with his pocket full of payoffs for Bible verses committed to heart—is evidence of love. The world around the little rock house, the universe in a drop of pond water at the bottom of the microscope, the *terra incognita* beyond the Blue Ridge, the whole shebang is for us to love because God loved the world before we, the world, loved God.

*　　　*　　　*

Lying on my stomach one June afternoon, watching two large, shiny black beetles make love, I smiled. I knew a secret. They, even they—with their pinpoint brains, busy making other beetles, publicly humping one another with abandon—were cherished. Maybe they were doing the dirty out of boredom, or perhaps in joyful obedience to the God who ordered, "Be fruitful and multiply."

Or maybe they were doing it out of a perverse need to be one on top of the other? Our loves are ambiguous, all mixed up with our will to power. Augustine forged a link between sin and sex, impugning sexuality for Christians. John Wesley thought that sinful willfulness, self-deceit and self-centeredness, inclination to dominate and to do evil don't kick in until puberty, but kick in they do. All of which is to say that one way or another, by nature or nurture, we are sinners who fall short of the goodness and glory of God (Rom. 3:23). Way short. Though I was made "in the image of God" (Gen. 1:27), in actuality, like Mark Twain said of himself, I'm more of a rough sketch.

All the more remarkable that God created the world and called it good. No South Carolinian disbelieves in original sin. We've been bad. Our grandparents, worse. We therefore, for any of our virtues, require redemption by something other than moral grit or government programs for human betterment. Another advantage of growing up guilty in Greenville.

As Kierkegaard said, "consciousness of sin is the way of entrance" into Christianity. Though we wouldn't dare talk about it at the Sunday dinner table, my people had much reason to be grateful that Jesus Christ saves sinners, only sinners (1 Tim. 1:15). Jesus Christ was crucified for saving people nobody thought could be saved, people nobody wanted saved (Rom. 3:23). Some sinners' sin is in being from South Carolina and others' sin is in praying, "God, I thank thee that I am not like those racist, right-wing, Republican, NRA Southern sinners."

Watching my boxer degut a dead chicken he stole from Uncle Charles's barn, I was humbled by the recognition that even this dog—dumbest ever there was, named "Captain," though captain of nothing—was loved by God in a way I could not.

So, that's the reason. We were put here, located in love, bred for the joy of knowing we, even in our sin and lostness, are owned. Our telos, our baptismally bestowed purpose, is to allow ourselves to be loved, to be lost and found, to say yes to the Yes that God has said to us.

When a pious kid smugly announced, just before pickup softball at fourth grade recess, "Last night I got saved. I went and give my life to Christ. I'm rede-e-e-emed," I wondered, *why would you boast?* You can't give something to somebody who already owns what's being given. All that smart-ass little Baptist had done was to say yes to the obvious, to admit to the way things were, to allow himself to be loved.

The world began with God preaching to the darkness, calling forth light. In love, God calls forth something out of nothing. God didn't stop loving on the sixth day of creation. Little is here on its own. Everything must be preached to, called for, evoked, summoned. For me, as for beetles or boxers, vocation initiates creation and keeps it going. The love that made the world, evoked the sun, moon, and stars, calls the pines to sway in the morning, teaches crickets to sing, and makes dead dogs to speak also refuses to leave us be.

To be sure, things are haunted, thick and mysterious, but they also speak, relate, reveal if you look closely and take some time with them. God, according to Genesis, loves to talk. If a poplar tree, or a dark, copulating beetle, a rotting, dead dog at the bottom of a well can reveal, well, what else might be sacramental? Chesterton said that materialism is perilous. Positivists are always in danger of being smacked by some weird phenomenon that shatters their secular, naturalistic belief that what we see is all there is.

"Only the One who created the world can create a Christian," said John Wesley, long before I met him. It takes a leap of faith to believe that God had a hand in the Grand Canyon or a Carolina wren. Even greater faith is to believe that the same God is breathing breath into dust, busy making humanity out of mud, evoking you.

Henry Fielding's Tom Jones says that nothing much happened to him during his first ten years of life. I, on the other hand, spent my first decade embraced by an uncanny sense of being watched, beckoned, summoned, a gate opening to I knew not where, moments when (in the words of David Bentley Hart) I was given "recognition of the sheer fortuity of being." That I have, on the whole, fond memories of my childhood is tribute to the skill of my mother in raising a happy enough child, despite deficits in finances and paternity. Give God some of the credit. A redemptive God loves nothing better than to counter unfortunate circumstances by calling us to be more than we could have been on our own.

By the beginning of my second decade I knew: something's afoot; someone knows my name; somebody's trying to get through.

2

Unwitting Call

The LORD God called unto Adam, . . . Where art thou? And
he said, I heard thy voice in the garden, and I was afraid.
(Genesis 3:9–10)

At the age of four, my older brother Bud suffered a bout of scar-
let fever. The Christmas before, he had received a toy toolbox
full of hammers, screwdrivers, and wrenches. When Bud's fever
finally broke, my mother decided that she could safely foray into
downtown Greenville. Bud was left in bed, watched over by our
imperious—beloved all the more because of her high-handed-
ness—family retainer, Sadie.

When Mother returned, she was stunned. A toy saw it may
have been, but the saw was enough for Bud to hack off the bed-
posts, and the claw hammer, also from the toy toolbox, adequate
for stripping the paper from the walls around his bed.

"That poor baby been so sick," said Sadie, "and he was having him such a good time, for the life of Jesus I just couldn't tell
him no."

"That was *uncalled for*," said Mother.

As pastor, college chaplain, bishop, and seminary professor, I've heard hundreds of accounts of *called-for* lives. In most, the call comes long before the person knows the Caller. A vocative God takes over enemy-held territory by flirting, teasing, courting, cajoling, darting from tree to tree, as Flannery O'Connor would say, rather than by frontal assault. Copulating beetles, the view from a barn, a defiant, revelatory poplar—a calling God is nothing if not resourceful. Still, if God's vocation can't be explained in many other ways, it's probably not the God who called light out of darkness, summoned little Samuel out of bed, or blinded Paul on the Damascus road. A fully comprehensible god can't ever be the God who calls for you.

Jean-Paul Sartre tells the story of a French student during World War II, in the Nazi occupation, who was torn between his sense of responsibility to care for his mother and his desire to leave her and join the French resistance. He sought the guidance of the town's priests. Each priest gave different advice. To Sartre, this priestly ambiguity showed the speciousness of Christian ethics. To counter the vagueness of God, Sartre offered the young man existentialism: "You are free, therefore choose . . . invent. No rule of general morality can show you what you ought to do . . . we ourselves decide our being." Ah, the modern way: heroically choose yourself free from all external attachments and responsibilities in order more tightly to tether yourself to yourself. Self-call.

"I did it my way" is evidence that one is attempting the uncalled-for life, on one's own, unaccountable, oblivious to any commanding, demanding external claim. It's up to us to give our lives a theme. I was born in 1946, as were Donald Trump, George W. Bush, and Bill Clinton. Also Jefferson Beauregard Sessions, whom I took to court in the Alabama anti-immigration fight. (Amid Jeff's valiant protection of Alabama's borders with Mexico and Syria, Jeff managed to find time to opine that I was a disgrace to Alabama Methodism.) More auspiciously, my natal year yielded Dolly Parton, Steven Spielberg, André the Giant, Pat Sajak, Barry Gibb, Jimmy Buffett, Cher, and Liza Minnelli. Not a shabby year, though I fail to see a common theme. Oh yes, 1946 is also the birth year of Ted Bundy, the most prolific (thirty-six victims) serial killer in America.

*   *   *

My adolescent attempt to make something of myself was Scouting. Secretary of State Rex Tillerson told a Scouting convention, "Will Willimon is one of my favorite writers," which thrilled me. Then Rex spoiled it by boasting, "I've read everything he has written." No way Rex would have had time to climb to the top of Exxon if he had done that much reading.

Rex was impressed by my confession (when I spoke at the hundredth anniversary of the Boy Scouts) that what I know about leadership I learned in Scouting. When a district superintendent told me, "Bishop, there is no way you are going to persuade the Conference into reorganization," I replied, "You clearly don't know to whom you are talking. I convinced a group of fellow twelve-year-olds—Camp Old Indian, near midnight on a Saturday in January, ten degrees and sleeting, no electricity—to go to the creek and wash the pots and pans from supper. *I am* a visionary, results-oriented, entrepreneurial, transformative leader!"

In claiming that the main thing I got out of Scouting was leadership, I was being less than truthful with Rex. The chief training I received in Scouting was an advanced course in works righteous-

ness and the cultivation of overweening ambition. Scouting's constant encouragement to climb the ranks, to accumulate merit badges, and to outshoot, outchop, outlearn, outfight, and (after "Taps") out-self-care everyone else kept ambitious male adolescents like me busy.

God and Country Award by twelve, Order of the Arrow (Brotherhood rank, no less) by thirteen, Eagle not long after, National Jamboree—I kept my mother busy ripping patches off my uniform and sewing on new ones as I ascended the ranks.

I wasn't any good at sports (blame my fatherless, rural childhood). Scouts was my sole way of climbing, though no junior high school girl has ever gone steady with a boy because he was an Eagle Scout.

I'm unsure of the roots of my youthful ambition. Watching my mother agonizing over her checkbook each evening—distraught over having to buy a new set of tires—may have made me determined to find some way to make enough money not to be anxious. I don't recall feeling insecure as a child, so I suppose that my compulsive ambition, though often hidden from public view, was due to the chief of the Seven Deadly Sins. If enough teachers tell you that you are "bright," you believe it. As a defense against your advances, girls call you "mature and responsible." There was nothing left for me but to earn a dozen merit badges a summer, write eighty books, and be a lifetime *pre*crastinator, a preacher whose sermon is always ready a week before it's due.

My senior year of college, when a letter was slid under my dormitory door, telling me that I was a Phi Beta Kappa, I thought, *I owe my ability to climb upward to the Order of the Arrow, Attakullakulla Lodge 185, Blue Ridge Council, Boy Scouts of America.*

A chief problem with ambitiousness is that if you are deeply ambitious, as I was bred to be, there are never enough achievements, accolades, or merit badges to satisfy. The morning after being awarded Eagle, I began work on the bronze palm to pin on my Eagle badge. Once I was elected president of the Junior Classical League at Greenville High, I began my campaign to be state president. *Excelsior!*

Insecurity is a bottomless pit. Each trophy is quickly tarnished. After being recognized as the top student in the eighth grade, I thought, *the Greenville school system must suck.* When I was elected president of the student body at Hughes Junior High School, the principal announced my election over the PA. As the student body halfheartedly applauded my ascension, I thought, *I want to be elected for being popular but have to settle for "mature and responsible."*

Trouble is, thirty-eight merit badges (seventeen more than are required to be an Eagle) don't add up to a life worth living.

Without knowing it, I longed to be called out, called upon, called for.

*   *   *

"Vocation," called for by God, is a term now used in print less than at any time since the mid-nineteenth century. The vocational assertion "It is [God] that hath made us, and not we ourselves" (Ps. 100:3) sounds odd, schooled as we are in the fiction that our lives are our exclusive possessions to use as we choose.

"Who am I?" or "Why am I here?" evokes in unison the officially sanctioned, widely held, governmentally subsidized creed: *I am self-fabricated, autonomous, my personal property, the sum of my astute choices and my heroic acts of detachment from anyone more important than me. I bow to no claim other than that to which I have freely consented. I'm the captain of my fate, master of my soul, author of the story that is me.*

Christians assert the un-American conviction that our lives are less interesting than the God who assigns us. To paraphrase Aquinas, we're contingent creatures. We're the moon, not the sun; our light is derivative, reflective of the Light of the World. The God who had the brilliant idea to breathe life into mud (Gen. 2:7) loans breath, but only for as long as God wills.

All sorts of lies keep us from knowing the truth of our contingency and dependency. The myth of self-invention underwrites the market that gives us fifty kinds of pizza and four hundred TV channels, and calls the resulting wasteland "freedom." Never have so many been so free to get so much of what they want yet have so little notion of the life worth wanting, making it impossible to choose themselves into the good life.

Augustine charged that our boasts of Promethean human freedom of choice are but the rattling of our chains, a failure truthfully to acknowledge our masters. In this supermarket of desire, endless, never really satisfied consumption is our fate.

I tell myself that I am free of externally imposed masters while failing to admit my serfdom to the most imperious of lords: *me.*

"What should I do with my life?" is the question universities program students to ask. Faculty lure students into abandoning family, tribe, and neighborhood, put them through a food court of courses called the curriculum, making it possible for them to waste huge amounts of time with their peers (who know as little of life as they) and asking them to choose "which courses I want to take," even though they lack both the experience and the wisdom to know what they want. The university serves a mobile, demanding market by teaching students to ask, "What should *I* do with *my* life?"

Modernity compels us to write the story that defines who we are, heroically to choose from a variety of possible plots.

Believing that most of the important things that define us are accidental, externally imposed, Christians believe the question is not "What do I want to do with me?" but rather "Which God am I worshiping and how is that God having his way with me?"

Now we come to my discovery of the God who discovered me.

My sophomore dream trip to Europe (envisioned as a twenty-four-hour-a-day, three-month bacchanal) was commandeered by God and made a comedy of vocation. By midsummer a blue VW Beetle (purchased at the factory the Nazis built at Wolfsburg) deposited us in Amsterdam. In the Rijksmuseum, while my buddies explored the city that knows no sin, I stood face-to-face with the paintings I'd only seen as slides in Constance Armitage's Art History 101. I wondered before a melancholy Rembrandt self-portrait, so real I had to look away. To my right, an older man intently studied a van Ruisdael. He looked familiar, but who would I know so far from home?

Dr. Marney! A week or so of gray beard, but there he was—Carlyle Marney. Six months before, Marney (as he preferred to be called) had come to Wofford College's annual Religious Emphasis Week. He spoke with his deep voice that sounded like God, if Yahweh had been a Baptist from Tennessee. He swore, even in sermons, and made outrageous comments meant to thrill sophomores like me. I had retained none of his sermons' content, except something about Marney's horse in the pasture, turning its head when Marney whistled. *Impenetrable metaphor for God?*

I hesitantly approached, "Dr. Marney?"

"Who the hell are you?" he replied, looking me up and down cautiously.

"Oh, just a student at Wofford where you spoke last spring."

"I was glad to see that Wofford finally has got some little black boys. 'Bout time," he said, grinning.

"Yessir. My class was the first to integrate."

Marney stood there, assessing me.

"Are you in Europe preaching?" I asked.

"I'm here *to recover the Jew*," he said, punching his finger into my chest. "Eight synagogues in five days. Rubbing my clean Christian nose in the ashes of the circumcised."

Very awkward pause.

"And you? Why are you here?" he demanded.

"Me? I'm just bumming around Europe with some guys, looking for girls, just having a good time."

"You take me for some kind of fool, boy? I've been a preacher long enough to know when somebody is lying."

"Uh, then I guess I don't know why I'm here," I stammered.

"Good! Maybe we can get somewhere. Unamuno: knowing that you don't know is the beginning of knowing. May I help?"

He grabbed my arm. "These Dutch have told me more truth than I can take in one afternoon. God, I need a drink. You?"

Marney led me down the steps, out the front door, and into the first bar outside the museum.

"Got bourbon?" he called to a waiter across the dim, smoky bar. "Doesn't need to be fine bourbon. This boy doesn't know the difference and I don't expect good mash this far from home. Two. Straight up."

Watching Marney fiddle with his pipe, I was excited, at last being taken somewhere dangerous.

"Now that you've got some liquor in you," he said after his first sip, "you ready to talk? No horseshit. Who brought you here? What's the reason you won't admit?"

Marney began tamping sweet-smelling tobacco into his pipe.

"Uh, I thought I was here just to see Europe. My first time and all. I really like art history . . ."

"You started this, barging in when I'm trying to come to terms with Abraham," mumbled Marney, accusingly, then settling back in his chair, closing his eyes as if he had heard nothing noteworthy.

"When you were speaking at Wofford, I got to thinking, or else I finally admitted to myself that I had been thinking, that maybe, I ought to think about applying for one of those Rockefeller grants for a trial year at seminary, but . . ."

Marney grinned as if he had finally figured me out. "Son, life's less monologue and more dialogue." I had awoken to an exam for which I had not studied.

"It's just I'm really bothered that I'd be thinking about seminary. It seems kinda crazy," I said nervously.

"Why crazy?" asked Marney, staring across the bar, feigning disinterest, puffing on his pipe.

I began a rambling narration. "I grew up without a father, you see. My father left us when . . ."

Marney shook his head. "No. Your daddy can abscond, die, disown, but everybody's got some daddy or another. I bet you went out and found one, didn't you? Besides, how the devil does not having a daddy explain you here, now? God's of the living, not the dead."

I was grateful for the table between us. I blurted, "You see, since I've been at college I've gotten to read Freud, and I'm thinking, 'maybe my fixation on God is just my compensation for my lack of a father while I was growing up.' Wish fulfillment, maybe."

"Probably," smirked Marney.

"My thinking about God is just my psychological reaction to my daddy being in prison and all?"

"Look," said Marney, laying aside his pipe and moving toward me across the table as if to grab hold, aggravated at having to explain the obvious. "Son, *God will use any handle God can get.*"

Too long a silence. Then I asked, "But, how can I figure out what's *God* and what's my own screwed-up background?"

In an exhale of smoke Marney pronounced, "Son, God will take advantage of any screwed-up background, crooked daddy, manipulative mama. Read the Scriptures, for God's sake! I swear, I've never known a preacher worth a damn who didn't have a bad mama or daddy problem. God can work with either. Be glad you only got one loss for God to take advantage of.

"Yep. I'm pretty sure God's got your name. Not the first time I've heard this story. You're nobody special. Got God's fingerprints all over it. You have time for me to have another one of these?" he said, pointing to his empty glass. "My good man," he shouted to the waiter. "This round, don't spoil it with ice. My protégé likes it straight. *Garçon, encore bourbon!*"

Sometime before dawn, tossing, turning on the dirty mattress in the fleabag monastic cell that three of us had rented for eight dollars a night, accompanied by the sound of some student puking in the shared toilet down the hall, I said the words that Paul surely prayed when God blinded him: *Why not somebody else? What kind of God would call somebody like me? But I don't want to be a Methodist preacher.*

Disregard my "Edenic" childhood. That night in Amsterdam was the birth of the accidental, initially humiliating, but eventually happy life that is not my own, summoned, made accountable to someone other than myself, answerable to an externally imposed claim.

On the seasick sail back to Wofford at the end of the summer I read Vonnegut's *On the Road*, carefully underlining a sentence as if it were Holy Writ: "Keep your hat on; we may end up miles from here."

3

Inadvertent Summons

In the year that king Uzziah died I saw also the Lord sitting upon a throne, high and lifted up. . . . Above it stood the seraphims: each one had six wings; with twain he covered his face, and with twain he covered his feet, and with twain he did fly. And one cried unto another, and said, Holy, holy, holy, is the LORD of hosts. . . . Then said I, Woe is me! for I am undone; because I am a man of unclean lips, and I dwell in the midst of a people of unclean lips: for mine eyes have seen the King, the LORD of hosts. Then flew one of the seraphims unto me, having a live coal in his hand, which he had taken with the tongs from off the altar: And he laid it upon my mouth, and said, Lo, this hath touched thy lips; and thine iniquity is taken away, and thy sin purged. Also I heard the voice of the Lord, saying, Whom shall I send, and who will go for us? Then said I, Here am I; send me. And he said, Go, and tell this people . . . (Isaiah 6:1–9)

In a rare lapse into autobiography, Isaiah dates his call, "In the year that king Uzziah died," leaving us to speculate why the death of the king was significant in the young prophet's vocation. Methodists adore this passage. Our Methodist national anthem is based on Isaiah 6, Dan Shutte's "Here I Am, Lord." Few Methodists make it through two stanzas of this hymn without volunteering to go evangelize Zulus or at least to shed a maudlin tear.

> Here I am, Lord, is it I, Lord? I have heard you calling in the night.... I will go, Lord, where you send me ... I ...

Note the prevalence of the first-person personal pronoun as vocation degenerates into volunteering. Rather than risky encounter with a summoning God, worship morphs into sappy songs, syrupy clichés on the screen, followed by the sharing of tiring details about our personal lives at the coffee hour. Christian preaching slides into "Come right over here and sit next to me. I'm dying to tell you all about myself," and theology becomes commentary on human experience of God rather than God. Interiority writ large.

Here I am, Lord overlooks a great gift of vocation: rescue from our overly cultivated subjectivity. Vocation's power, said Hermann Hesse, is when "the soul is awakened . . . , so that instead of dreams and presentiments from within a summons comes from without," and an external relation "presents itself and makes its claim."

As Kierkegaard said, true knowledge of God "does not arise from any human heart." At its best, worship is ecstatic (Greek: *ekstasis*, "to stand outside oneself"), a nearly impossible feat for us modern, Western people.

Emerson left urbane Boston Transcendentalism because he came to see that Transcendentalism's cultivation of subjectivity stifled abolitionist action against American slavery. Isaiah 6 shows notoriously little interest in interiority and is loath to claim too much for human relationships to underscore that the most determinative of all relationships is with God. What did Uzziah's demise have to do with Isaiah's momentous encounter with the Lord? Had Uzziah been a father figure to young Isaiah?

We are conditioned to assume that the human, historical context is always a better explanation than God—if Isaiah *saw also the Lord sitting upon a throne, high and lifted up*, his vision must be due to some glitch in his psyche or perhaps a problem with Mom and Dad. Isaiah says nothing more about the end of Uzziah's reign. Administrations come and go—who cares? What's happening inside Isaiah or his social/historical context is less significant than what is happening outside. There is no Isaiah there until the divine address, *Who will go for us?*

*　　*　　*

"It is God that hath made us, and not we ourselves" (Ps. 100:3). Another shiny quarter memorization verse in Sunday school. What a relief to know that God likes to make things; you can't devise yourself from scratch.

"The best part of being a Lutheran," explained a young Canadian, "is baptism, when the church just tells you who you are. I've spent my whole life trying to figure out which path to take. So at my baptism the church doused me and said, 'Here's who God meant you to be, this is the life you were created to live.'"

That we are not self-made implies that we are God's property, to be called for as God pleases. In the New Testament, "calling" or "vocation" refers to discipleship rather than employment. We can be called to "eternal life" (1 Tim. 6:12) or into fellowship with Christ (1 Cor. 1:9), out of darkness into light (1 Pet. 2:9), and into right relationship with God (Rom. 8:30), but not to a career. Paul was a tentmaker (Acts 18:3), but nowhere is Paul "called" to be a tentmaker. Tentmaking put bread on the table, justification enough for Paul to give it his best.

Humans have careers; vocation is what God does.

"Mythologist" Joseph Campbell famously defines vocation as "following your bliss." Frederick Buechner similarly says vocation is "where your deep gladness and the world's deep hunger meet." Bliss is made suspect by Jesus Christ—who casts fire on the earth (Luke 12:49), turning father against son (Luke 12:53), bringing not peace but a sword (Matt. 10:34). Better than flaccid gladness, Jesus brings enlistment, incendiary vocation in mission that sometimes destroys bliss. Ask Paul.

"I like working with people, therefore . . ." or "I'm good with words, so naturally . . ." is not the way of vocation. How about nursing sick people? No? That doesn't appeal? Hey, what about advertising?

Vocation is not evoked by your bundle of need and desire. Vocation is what God wants from you whereby your life is transformed into a consequence of God's redemption of the world. Look no further than Jesus's disciples—remarkably mediocre, untalented, lackluster yokels—to see that innate talent or inner yearning has less to do with vocation than God's thing for redeeming lives by assigning us something to do for God.

In his revealingly titled *Let Your Life Speak*, Parker Palmer charges that the church's view of vocation is "an act of violence toward ourselves," in which a vision "is forced on the self from without rather than grown from within." Palmer's conventionally American "voice" arises from himself: "Before I can tell my life what I want to do with it, I must listen to my life telling me who I am."

Without a Christ who summons, Palmer's sweet voice within is the best we can muster. But who, intently listening to his or her own subjectivity, risks anything as costly and crazy as God routinely demands?

"Mary, how did you decide, by listening to your life, to become pregnant out of wedlock, have a sword pierce your soul, and bear the crucified Son of God into the world?"

See what I mean?

Vocation is not an inner inclination awaiting discovery by rooting around in the recesses of the ego. As Jesus succinctly says, "Ye have not chosen me, but I have chosen you, and ordained you, that ye should go and bring forth fruit" (John 15:16).

My adolescent, long-night-in-Amsterdam question, "What kind of God would choose someone like me?" is answered by Scripture. The God who chose Israel and the church is a sucker for the likes of me. You can look it up. Jesus begins his work not by a solo dive into ministry but by putting the finger on a dozen knuckleheads and commissioning them to do what he wants done in the world, calling for them in order that they "should go and bring forth fruit."

God's got some form of discipleship in mind for everybody. Everyone can expect vocation—that peculiar way God uses you, creation of God, in God's salvation of the world. One of the happiest aspects of my happy pastoral life is watching the ways in which God calls—to write letters to the incarcerated, to do time on the church finance committee, to empty the bedpans of those in need, to raise a couple of godly children, to set a good table for the hungry, or to be a public school teacher. While my peculiar vocation is to be a preacher, the first person who comes to my mind when I hear "vocation" is Oscar Dantzler, custodian of Duke Chapel. My chief achievement, in twenty years there, was to convince Oscar that God wanted him to care for God's house at Duke and to be the point man in God's hospitality to everyone.

On a recent Sunday, while it was still dark, Oscar opened the chapel and readied the building for the proper worship of God so he would be ready by ten-thirty to take his place at the front door to welcome all.

At the Northside UMC Wednesday morning prayer breakfast (God and a sausage biscuit at an ungodly hour), I piously asked the assembled laity, "Pray for Mary. Johnny was booked last night. DUI. I'm going to see what I can do to get him out. Mary's had a time with that boy."

"How much you know about alcoholism?" said one of the men, unimpressed by my pastoral care.

"Where you going to get the money for bail?" asked another. "We'll go with you. Take this off the prayer list. We can handle it."

The three of us walked into the bowels of the jail, where we saw a frightened youth, huddled in the corner of a cell, weeping.

"Son, how long have you had a problem with alcohol?" one of the men asked through the bars.

"Uh, I wouldn't say I have 'a problem,'" Johnny replied.

"Let me rephrase that. How long have you been lying about your problem? Son, I've learned a lot about booze the hard way. Had that monkey on my back since I was in the army. I can show you the way out."

"We're springing you," said another, who was a lawyer. "And you come home with me. Our kids are out of the house. Your mama's got enough on her already. I'd love to have somebody to watch Clemson football with."

A vocative God showing off.

*   *   *

And, yes, vocation may lead to self-deceit. When I raised questions about an administrator's poor performance, she snapped back as feistily as a schnauzer, "I'm sure that Jesus called me to this job."

Nothing so easily shuts up a critic, or covers for self-deception, as blaming your inadequacies on the poor vocational judgment of Jesus.

A particularly dangerous temptation for clergy like me is to think that we've tamed ambition by following a downwardly mobile vocation like Christian ministry. William James said that self-aggrandizing ambition comes in three ways: material (moneygrubbing), social (honor and acclaim), and spiritual. Of course, James suspects spiritual self-seeking to be the most deceitful; spiritual upward mobility is often compensation for failing at other types of ambition and therefore liable to breed invidious comparison: "God, I thank thee, that I am not as other men are" (Luke 18:11).

Sharing James's suspicion of spiritual self-seeking is one reason why I mistrust the *au courant* enthusiasm for "Christian practices," the latest iteration of our history of eager-beaver spiritual self-promotion. Although Sabbath keeping, contemplative prayer, and spiritual centering promise to purge our self-seeking, there's more than a whiff of works-righteous asceticism in these practices designed to get a vocative, living God off our backs.

Don't forget that Paul's "the good that I would I do not. . . . Who shall deliver me from the body of this death?" (Rom. 7:19, 24) was made *after* his Damascus road call.

*   *   *

Augustine said that his youthful promiscuity, being "in love with love," was a primary way he unconsciously kept God at bay. A chief barricade against Jesus's calling for me was my "daddy problem," exposed and disarmed in Amsterdam by Marney. Daddy issues have given rise to some of the world's great literature. In the *Odyssey*, after introducing his "wandered widely" hero Odysseus, Homer surprisingly focuses upon Odysseus's left-behind son, Telemachus. Telemachus was an infant when daddy sailed off for glory in Troy. Now in his twenties, Telemachus mopes around the palace bemoaning the disastrous effects of his father's two-decade absence. His patrimony wasted by the suitors who hanker after his mother, his daddy's kingdom in a mess, and mom, Penelope, sulking alone.

Strange that Homer begins a story extolling the exploits of the father by focusing upon the son he abandoned. Eventually, Homer sends Odysseus to Hades, where he sees the error of his vainglorious wandering, returns home, slays the suitors, and resumes his marital state, though we doubt that Odysseus and the son he abandoned live happily ever after.

When I first read the *Odyssey* as a Wofford freshman, I thought, *I am Telemachus.*

Among the important things never mentioned at the wide-ranging Sunday dinner conversations among the Willimons was the familial embarrassment of my father.

"What am I to say when they ask, 'Where's your father?'"

My mother's most detailed response: "Just say that your father doesn't live here anymore." *That's a relief. At least there was a time when I had a father.* I mined my memory for some shred of recollection. I remembered climbing into a man's lap and watching him fill his pipe with tobacco. There was also the scratch of whiskers. Then there was a memory of being in Skelton's grocery store with a man with a pipe who pulled a cold "dope" out of the cooler and handed it to me. When he did, someone in the store asked, "A Coakercoler for your grandson, right, Bob?"

The man who had given me the drink replied, "Go to hell. That's my *son!*"

Beyond that, nothing.

There was a tobacco humidor with pipes on the living room shelves. "Was that Daddy's?" I asked.

"Yes" was all I got. Sniffing the amber-colored jar provided my sole tangible confirmation of paternity.

One day, alone, rummaging in the desk I was forbidden to open, I found a letter from the warden of the US prison in Atlanta. "To whom it may concern: The prison record of Robert C. Willimon has been exemplary." *How would I live up to Daddy's success as a convict?*

Working as a teenage gofer in the Orderest Mattress Factory in Greenville, I joined the others in picking on the floor manager (made minor overseer for no other reason than he was white). The ignorant, toothless man snarled a curse everyone heard: "You can't say nothin' to me! Your daddy was a damn thief!"

My career as a moralist ended by a father I hardly knew, robbed of self-righteousness before I could use it.

As student body president of Hughes Junior High, I gave a speech one night to the PTA. The editor of the *Greenville News* came up afterward and said, "You've sure got that Willimon gift of gab. Who's your daddy, Charles or Gene?"

I gulped. "Robert was my father."

"No kidding? Didn't know Bob had a boy as young as you."

He bent down and whispered, "Bob could talk a preacher into breaking the Ten Commandments. That son of a bitch talked me out of ten thousand dollars. Left town. Never paid back a cent." *Another profession, banking, closed to me forever.*

"But I'll tell you this," he went on. "If your daddy walked right through that door and said, 'Bill, give me ten thousand dollars. I've got a great idea that'll make you rich,' I would whip out my checkbook. God-a-mighty, what a man with words!"

In the ninth grade, with Bev Beckwith at my first formal dance, I whispered over her low-cut formal, "Your father doesn't like me."

She replied, "That's not true. I told him how nice you are. He likes you; it's your daddy he hates."

Knowing my intentions, I asked, "So what did you tell your father was nice about me?"

That same year I was assigned the role of Enoch Snow Jr. in the school production of *Carousel*. My only line came when I held up my nose and contemptuously sneered at Louise Bigelow, "You're father was a *thief*!" Ironic, right?

*   *   *

One day in high school I asked an aunt to violate family law and "tell me about Daddy."

Here's what she told me: When Harry and Bud were young, my father committed bank fraud, or bank robbery, or maybe both; it's hard to remember exactly. At the time, Daddy was reputed to have more liens against him for unpaid bills than anybody in the history of Greenville. His Greenville Pickens Speedway, road construction company, and a dozen other brilliant ideas busted. He was sent to the federal pen in Atlanta, or maybe the one in Indiana, at one time or another; it's hard to remember.

Through it all, my mother stood by, awaiting his return. Daddy was released from jail and returned to the Willimon place. Nine months later, even though he and my mother were in their forties, I was born. Alas, my father's troubles resumed, and, after some misdeed that broke the proverbial camel's back, one Sunday the family had a meeting and decided it would be better for all if my father would leave.

Leave?

Mother was consulted and agreed, after being told that the family would look after me, my brother, and sister. Daddy was written out of the will and my brother Bud, my sister Harriet, and I received the three-hundred-acre inheritance that would have gone to my father. My mother's sole condition was that no one ever speak of my father because "this little boy ought not grow up with that burden."

Everyone kept that promise.

It's all absurd, of course, dark and sublime Faulknerian Southern Gothic worthy of Carson McCullers, Toni Morrison, or maybe even Eudora Welty. But people handled things differently back then. What was left of a family's fictional dignity must ruthlessly be preserved. Adults, having made a mess of so much, prided themselves in their ability not to mention a few things that were deemed too unpleasant to lay upon a child. Their obfuscation produced a large void in my Eden.

I was twenty-two, at a family wedding in Raleigh, when my aunt Alice came into the motel room where we were gathered and asked, "Would you like to meet your father?"

"Yes, I guess."

Led into an adjoining room, I was greeted by an older man, smoking a pipe. We shook hands. All I saw was an aging relative for whom I had no more feeling than for a distant cousin.

"I hear you have done right well for yourself," he said with a twinkle in his eye. "Hear you know how to make a dollar." *I have heard you are good at talking people out of money! Son, you make me proud.*

I recalled that he was reputed to be a great liar. The only truth in his first words to me were "You have done right well for yourself." Of course, as he would later reassure me, leaving was not his idea and "your mother is a wonderful person." I eventually learned that he had remarried a couple of times, even though he had never gotten around to divorcing my mother (there's little time for paperwork when you are on the lam from creditors). Restaurants were built and lost, a children's game company, horseshoe foundry, and other brilliant schemes came to naught.

According to my aunt Ann, a prison psychiatrist diagnosed Daddy as suffering from "delusions of grandeur." God had afflicted my father with the psychological condition that leads to robbing banks.

In my first church in Clinton, South Carolina, I paid a pastoral visit to Miss Agnes (who had been my mother's roommate at Winthrop). "Willie, it seems like only yesterday that you were born!" she said after serving iced tea. "I remember visiting Ruby when she was expecting you. A terrible year, that was. She didn't care if she lived or died. Hair turned snow white during those nine months."

My nativity a "terrible year"?

"You can't expect her to have been happy about it. A forty-year-old woman surprised by a baby," she said with a dismissive little laugh as she offered me a cookie. "Still, I understand that you have brought her happiness. That's nice."

There you have it: I the accident, the firstfruits postprison. That's why I'm uneasy with the term "planned parenthood" and thank God that abortion wasn't readily available in 1946. God be praised for Bible stories of embarrassing pregnancies from Sarah, Hagar, and Mary. I'm also grateful that the best of the New Testament was written in jail, though there is no record that any of it was penned after a bank heist. And, while I'm counting blessings, thanks to a God who is raiser of the dead, redeemer of mistakes, jokester to the devil. Read your Bible. "But when it pleased God, who separated me from my mother's womb, and called me by his grace, to reveal his Son in me, that I might preach him among the heathen . . ." (Gal. 1:15–16).

If I could have mustered resentment against my father, or the family who cast him out, or their vast conspiracy of silence, I could have tested my obedience to Jesus's command to forgive enemies. I could be the courageous victim who clenched his fist and overcame all. Alas, my lack of attachment to my unknown father produced too little antipathy for me to get over. I do believe that my father improved my biblical interpretation. Saint Paul did jail time, so did our Lord.

You can learn Greek, but if your old man hasn't been a convict, I brag to seminarians, vast portions of the New Testament will be incomprehensible.

Friend Stanley Hauerwas says that he is constitutionally unsuited to be a Christian, even if he is from Texas. Due to the manner of my birth, Christian was the only profession open to me. This faith revels in embarrassing births—jailbird disciples and absentee, inept fathers are the rule.

A Duke student once asked, "How do you write so much?"

Misunderstanding, I responded, "Why so many books? Well, I was born into an extended, though Gothic, Southern family. My father was convicted of bank robbery and sent to jail, and I was born nine months after he got out. Then the family banished him so I never really had a father, which surely accounts for my compulsive need constantly to produce and to prove myself and . . ."

"Er, uh," the student responded. "I meant, like, do you use note cards, or do you just write it out as you go?"

The only photograph I have of my father was taken when he was five. He sits in the lap of Uncle Tom Fowler, the bearded, ancient mountaineer who watched over the Willimon summer retreat at Rich Mountain. Uncle Tom is erect, dignified and sitting in the chair holding a blond, booted child wearing a little bowler hat cocked to the right. The child squints like Willimons do, staring at the viewer with smart-assed self-assurance rarely seen in five-year-olds, smoking a cigar.

What if the tot with the cigar had known that his family would spend large amounts of money vainly trying to fix him and spring him out of jail, and finally disinherit him when he messed up one time too many? And then he sired me.

I think my father would still have sat there squinting confidently, preternaturally sure of his capabilities, looking upon everyone as an easy mark, hat cocked smartly, staring down the future like he owned it, aged five, smoking a cigar.

*   *   *

Marney was right: everybody's got a daddy, one way or the other. Without the church, God only knows where I would have found surrogate daddies. When I was ten, my mother deposited me at Buncombe Street Methodist (founded long before H. L. Mencken invented "bunkum") every Thursday afternoon for the church membership class. I retained nothing about Methodism from that class. My confirmation occurred not in the church sanctuary on a Sunday but rather in the parking lot on Thursday before Holy Week. On Palm Sunday we were to be joined to the church. The bulletin that Sunday was to feature a photo of the class lined up on the steps in front of the Ionic columns of Buncombe Street. (The facade earned the church a nickname, Jesus First National Bank.)

Thursday, I was greeted by the woman who commanded the confirmands: "Where's your tie?"

I froze.

"You were told to wear a tie. We're taking the confirmands' photo. There's a photographer—*a professional*. Dr. Herbert is to have his picture taken with the class—*the preacher.*" She waved her hand over the assembled righteous. "Every boy has a tie. Even Stanley Starnes. See? You were told."

Words failed. I wheeled around and dashed out the door to the back parking lot. I would post myself at the preacher's parking space, head him off, confess my sin, and humbly bow out of the picture.

Sure enough, there was Dr. Herbert, pulling his light blue Plymouth into the space. I breathlessly ran up and blurted, "Dr. Herbert, you don't know me but I'm William Willimon, and I didn't hear that we were supposed to have a tie, or I forgot, or maybe my mother didn't tell me, and I don't want to be in the picture anyway and . . ."

Dr. Herbert, with his stained-glass bass voice, replied, "Tie? Why on earth would you be wearing a tie? I am wearing a tie because I'm a pastor and I am forced to wear a tie. I'm unaware that you have had theological training."

All I've had is this dumb class.

"Are you not preparing yourself for membership in the Methodist Church?" he continued.

"Yessir."

"Well, son, I know more about these matters than anyone present, and I'm certain that there are no requirements in Methodism for ties to be worn in order to join the church. No record of our Lord ever having worn a tie, and I know Scripture. Come along. The whole point of these ceremonials is to put you in the picture."

He led me back into the darkened hall toward the primary classroom, where the others were detained.

"Everyone's here," reported the woman in charge. "Nearly everyone has dressed for the photograph, as they were told. Even Stanley Starnes."

My heart stopped.

"What a beautiful group!" exclaimed Dr. Herbert. "I have one request before we go out and take our place on the church steps. Boys, please, no ties on a Thursday. Only I can wear a tie in church on a weekday. Such are the rules of our Connection. You may wear them if you must on Sunday. Please remove your ties. Let's take that picture."

God is like Dr. Herbert, without the Plymouth.

*   *   *

God commanded father Abraham to sacrifice his son Isaac in order to test Abraham's fidelity. In my case, sacrifice was reversed. Because a boy without a daddy is fair game, I had to give up a few false fathers to be faithful to the vocation of the Father. I could go on, but as Mark Rothko says, there's more power in telling little than in telling all.

Even false father substitutes can be used by a redemptive God. The world into which I was born, with the woods and summer mornings, was close to Eden—if you overlooked the legally enforced white supremacy. Yet later or sooner everybody must grow up, face the imperfections, get his or her nose rubbed in history, and thereby be forced out of the garden by an angel with a flaming sword.

During Marney's week at Wofford my sophomore year, in a dormitory discussion with students, Marney mentioned the garden of Eden. A smart-mouthed religion major scoffed, "That's not a real, historical place. Eden's just a myth."

"The hell you say!" shot back Marney. "I can even tell you the garden's exact location: 136 Elm Street, Knoxville, Tennessee."

What?

"That's where my mama gave me a dollar to go buy eggs and milk but on the way I got detoured by the candy store." Marney tamped his pipe. "The candy looked good to eat. I ate the whole of it on the way home. Was so ashamed I hid in the closet. It was there she found me just before suppertime. She asked God's questions for him, 'Where are you? Who told you? What have you done?'"

*   *   *

It helped that just about everyone in my generation had parent problems. Our parents had lied to us about Vietnam and civil rights. If you were a student in the sixties and free of friction with your elders, you weren't showing up for work.

Being a Christian complexified the already conflicted inter-action between generations—Jesus urged us to hate our mothers (Luke 14:26), then turned around and commanded us to love our enemies (Matt. 5:44).

One Sunday evening a fellow campus troublemaker barged in my dorm room in Shipp Hall, saying, "Give me a cigarette. Guess who I just sat across from on the flight from DC to Greenville/Spartanburg? Martin Luther Damn King! Just like he looks on TV. He slumped in his seat as soon as he got on the plane. Looked real tired. So I didn't bother him. Finally I got up the nerve to speak.

"'Dr. King, it's an honor to meet you. I'm active at my college, Wofford, in the movement. I'm coming from a training session in Washington. I really appreciate what you are doing.'"

"Unbelievable!" I exclaimed. "What did Dr. King say to you?"

"Nothing. So I said, 'Dr. King, my father is a farmer in low-country South Carolina. He's such a racist. I have tried to talk to him, tried to explain why the fight for racial justice is so important. But he says terrible things. I'm not going home for Thanksgiving because I don't want anything to do with such a redneck, racist old fool. His . . .'

"Dr. King lunged across the aisle, grabbed my arm, and said in a voice loud enough to wake the whole plane, 'You got to love your daddy!' Then he went back to sleep until we landed."

*   *   *

A decade later, my talk with Marney had set in motion a string of accidents that landed me back in Greenville. I was appointed pastor to a forlorn congregation that was planted by Buncombe Street Church when I was a child. By then my father had shown up in town once or twice, unannounced. We met for coffee, but Patsy and I told neither Harriet nor William about their long-gone grandfather because it seemed a dishonor to Mother.

As he was dying of cancer, visiting us was his way of "settling my debts"—an absurd supposition for a man who owed everybody. How, in God's name, was he going to repay me? We would look ridiculous, a dying old man and his middle-aged son at last attending the Boy Scout Troop Nine Father-Son Banquet.

My brother Bud cared for him and footed the bill for Daddy's last days. Toward the end, I phoned the hospital. A nurse answered. "Oh, Billy? He's so proud of you. Talks about you all the time. I think it's terrible the way your brother has taken all of Robert's money while he's been in the hospital. Your father is just the sweetest person, isn't he?"

Weak and dying, Daddy still had the "Willimon gift of gab." Though his body was failing him, his prevaricatory skill did not.

It was Christmas Eve 1981. Northside United Methodist Church had a rough ride the years prior to my arrival as their new pastor. Things were so bad they found neither the funds nor the enthusiasm even for a Christmas service the previous year. The dispirited congregation needed one undeniable success. Even if I singlehandedly had to mold the candles, grow the poinsettias, and falsetto-croon "O Holy Night," by God my first Northside Christmas would be a candlelight extravaganza of Yuletide emotion.

As I was putting the finishing touches on my sermon for that night's service, my brother called.

"Daddy just died."

The father I barely knew selects that night—my biggest night at my new church—for his exit, this time leaving for good. As we drove to church that night, I was ashamed of my lack of response. Though I tried to lament the tragedy of it all, my grief was no greater than that of a kid staring at a speckled hound at the bottom of the dry well. We hurried into church. I put on my robe, pulled tight the cincture, directed the candles to be lit, and formed the choir for the introit—"O Come, All Ye Faithful" instead of my preference, "In the Bleak Midwinter."

That's church for you. Church forces us to march in and sing even when we're not in a singing mood, not feeling faithful, and "joyful and triumphant" is not us. Church doesn't wait for you to have the proper motivation for worship in order to call you to worship. And there are so many times, when you have been called to be a pastor, that you don't feel like being a pastor but still must act the part. You may be in pain, may be in over your head emotionally and theologically. Though you are supposed to be an expert in helping others to grieve, you may not know how publicly to mark your own loss. As a pastor, your personal problems take a backseat to the needs of others. You're the only pastor they have, and Christmas comes but once a year. So you pull tight the cincture and pray, "God, who got me into this, give me the hardheaded determination to get through it." You go out and act like their pastor even when you don't want to.

When seminarians plead for graciousness for "personal reasons," when they are late with some class assignment because an aunt whom "I revered as if she were my grandmother" departed or they are suffering a bout of depression, I think, *Clergy who are not periodically depressed have either given up too soon or expect too little of Jesus. You can't stand up on Sunday and say, "Nothing would have pleased me more than to have a sermon for you but first it was one thing and then another so we're going to break up into discussion groups. Then we'll pool our collective ignorance and call that today's sermon."*

I'd get fired for saying this to a student, but even the dean can't keep me from thinking it.

That Christmas Eve at sad Northside, as at many other times and churches, I practiced the art of pastoral repression in service to my vocation. I stood up and played the preacher. Don't accuse me of deceit or denial—that night I was almost grateful for having something to pray over other than myself, pleased that baptism had given me a church family more messed up than my own, glad that a pregnant virgin is more newsworthy than a son unable properly to grieve the death of a failure at fatherhood.

I wasn't a hapless victim of poorly thought-out paternity or betrayals by bogus father figures who took advantage of my vulnerability. I was privileged to have been called for, compelled by my vocation to suck it up, take a deep breath, and stand and deliver, lay some Bible verse on them that would help them make it through the night. There was only me to say the divine words they couldn't say to themselves. Somebody's got to deliver the news, the good news for all who dwell in the land of darkness, whether it be east of Eden or on the north side of Greenville. Even though we "prefer darkness rather than light" (John 1), God incarnates anyway:

And the Word became flesh and dwelt among us . . .

In each of our histories, there is regret and unfinished business. The world, as good as it is, is never enough. Not enough time, not enough room for complete redemption or full reparation. Even God Almighty shares one limitation with us finite humans, said Aquinas: Even God cannot make our past not to have been. No retrieving the lost days, no recalling just the right Bible verse to make the fix, no taking back the thoughtless word.

You can't. That's when you give thanks that the Word, the eternal Logos, became flesh, our flesh, and moved in with us. God refused to stay spiritual. The Word intrudes with words we cannot say to ourselves, Light shines in our darkness. God so loved the world in all of its screwedupness and regret. There's only us to tell the story. We step forward, anyhow. We sing. *O come, all you faithful.* Come on, all you unfaithful. Let's adore him anyway.

And wonder above wonders, in a dejected little church that nobody has heard of on ironically named Summit Drive in Greenville, damn South Carolina, with an emotionally inept preacher without even the grace to mourn his departed thief of a father, *God with Us.* Alpha and Omega enters our finitude, incarnating into our misspent histories.

Thank God, God loves to talk. *Gloria in excelsis Deo.*

In the year that my father died, I saw the Lord, not high and lifted among the seraphim, but down and dirty with us on Summit Drive. The death of my father, like the death of King Uzziah, had nothing to do with it. It was more that God is determined to be with us, showing up as a baby of embarrassing paternal circumstances, born, as are we, from a woman's loins, a child needing the warmth and nurture of a thoroughly flawed human family.

An odd birth, an absent father, God come to those of unclean lips who could not come to God. Go ahead, Lord, live dangerously: *send me.*

4

Unexpected Church

I beseech Euodia, and beseech Syntyche, that they be of the same mind in the Lord. . . . Help those women which laboured with me in the gospel, with Clement also, and with other my fellow-labourers, whose names are in the book of life. (Philippians 4:2–3)

One June night, 1968, I sprawled at the base of the Reverend Benjamin Wofford's tombstone at the center of the campus staring at stars, imbibing with a friend. In two days our college careers would end and we would be off, he to a master's in English lit, I to divinity. How long would I last? Would Yalies look down on me because I was from a hick college in the South? Would I be trapped among theology nerds who didn't know how to have a good time?

My friend listened to my lament, then, as the sun rose over Spartanburg, said, "Get used to it. You've just been given fifty-to-life in the church. A month of Sundays. A Methodist preacher is all you will ever be."

At least I'll have God to blame for my failures.

Luther told clergy that ordination is not based on merit but on election by a God who is a sucker for "sinners, evil persons, fools and weaklings," that is, *the God of the church.*

In my early days, as I clambered up the wall for my escape to God, there were always inmates attempting to pull me back to the safety of bourgeois conformity, thinking I would be shot down by the mediocrity of Methodism. The morning after my induction into Phi Beta Kappa in 1968, my favorite professor said, "Really now, ought not you rethink seminary? You could do better." When I turned my back on Duke tenure to be pastor at sad Northside, the dean predicted, "The Methodist Church punishes mavericks whether of the right or the left. You'll regret this."

And when I left Duke Chapel to be a 'Bama bishop in 2004, a revered faculty friend shook his head. "What a waste. How will you endure the banality?"

Throughout my ministry, none asked, *Have you got the right stuff to consort with the bride of Christ?* My alluring tempters whispered, *Waste not your love on that compromised tart.*

It has been my peculiar vocation to have my life tethered to the corrupted bride of Christ, the crucified, full-of-holes body of Christ, yoked to God's grand, visible lapse of good judgment—*the Methodist Church.*

As bishop, my most somber duty was to take away the credentials of clergy calling it quits. Never has a pastor thrown in the towel from being fed up with Jesus, despite Jesus's demands being notoriously excessive. What kills clergy is the church.

If Jesus were a disembodied spirit, everybody would adore him. Novelist Jay Parini notes, "Bad luck is . . . part of what it means to have a body. Without a body, there could be no misfortune." Plato boasted that philosophy hefts us out of our decaying bodies through serene philosophical contemplation—bodies are the hard part of being human.

Salvation is conversion into the knowledge that we are saved as a body, a group, *the church*, or saved not at all. "He did not come to disembodied angels. He came to us" (Heb. 2:16–18, paraphrased).

After I left academia, a frequent Alabama question was, "What do you miss most in the university, compared with your new life as church bureaucrat?"

"I miss the Duke Office of Admissions, which ensured that I would never be forced to work with anyone unlike me. Sure, we had cultural and racial differences, but all of us shared the same gifts for manipulating the American educational system to our personal advancement. It was wonderful. Every day on the Duke campus without a really nasty disagreement.

"Church, on the other hand, is notoriously nonselective. Jesus prohibits Methodists having an admissions committee. You can choose friends, but you can't choose with whom to be church. Bishops are forced to work with anybody Jesus drags in the door."

Church can never be limited to me and my best buddies huddled around the blessed Eucharist because, as Henri Nouwen noted, church is constituted not by "family tie, or social or economic equality, or shared oppression or complaint, or mutual attraction, but the divine call. The Christian community is not the result of human effort. God has made us into his people by calling us."

I've seen schools kick faculty off the island for boorishness, insensitivity, or stubbornness, but unlike academia, in church Jesus makes us put up with one another even as our Lord puts up with us (Eph. 4:2). Flannery O'Connor said that she was happily Catholic because when she went to Mass at her little parish in Manhattan, she always saw a few people she knew—and many more whom she thanked God she didn't know. Like the blind man healed by Jesus (Mark 8:24), it takes a while to move from seeing people as trees walking to looking at them as beloved members of the body of Christ. A disembodied, docetic Jesus would be easier to worship than the Christ who takes up room in the world as the United Methodist Church, Inc. But it wouldn't be salvation in the name of Jesus.

I am a congenital believer. Resurrection? *Credo.* Virgin birth? No problem. *Homoousion, homoiousion,* I can swing either way. Yet to believe that the Son of God loved, died for, rose, and enlisted the likes of *me,* conditioning my eternal fate to Methodism, strains even my credulity.

✳   ✳   ✳

My clerical colleague Saint Paul testifies to the kenotic glory of Christ, calling in a most impressive theological artillery: "Christ

Jesus, who, though he was in the form of God, . . . emptied himself . . . and became obedient to the point of death. . . . Therefore God also highly exalted him . . . so that at the name of Jesus every knee should bend . . . and every tongue should confess that Jesus Christ is Lord" (Phil. 2:6–11 NRSV).

Here's the grandeur, the full sweep of orthodox theology, Paul's earliest and most extravagant christological acclamation. Then, after the glory, as if he has finally summoned the courage to say what's really bugging him, Paul explodes: "Euodia! Syntyche! Behave! Stop fighting. Damn it! Be reconciled!"

My 'Bama management coach taught me, "When reprimanding a subordinate, never put it in writing." Yet here, in the middle of his most sublime theology, Paul calls out—*in an open letter*—two saints, Euodia and Syntyche. Paul has written to First Church Philippi that they are Christ's answer to what's wrong with the world. They are saved, numbered among the saints in glory. And then, without warning or explanation, Paul slams—*by name*—two squabbling laypersons. What's this?

Church!

It's Sunday and I'm putting finishing touches on my sermon on Philippians 2, a deft exposition of the preexistence of Christ and its implications for people who drive Volvos. My study door bursts open, a prepubescent acolyte yells, "Preacher, come quick! Old lady Syntyche and Ms. Euodia are squared off in the sacristy over whether it's carnations or mums for Epiphany!"

Pastors give our lives to Jesus, only to have him shackle us to Euodia and Syntyche.

When I'm declared king of Methodism, which may happen any day, I'll make required reading *The Cost of Discipleship*. Bonhoeffer notes that no truth or doctrine "needs a space for itself." Disembodied abstractions can be admired but cannot be followed, and Jesus wants "living people who follow him." The church, yes, even the United Methodist Church, is the way the risen Christ is visibly, publicly present. "Christ invades the life of the world" and "conquers territory" bodily, including the enemy-held territory called me.

Jesus didn't come to tell us some truth; he said, "*I am* the truth," truth personal, embodied, in motion (John 14:6). A disembodied Christ wouldn't be Jesus. Out of love for him, we take upon ourselves his body, which, any pastor could tell you, requires heavy lifting.

When asked if I could help lift the comatose body of one of my church members who was in the last stages of dying from AIDS, I immediately took charge: "Sure, lift from the torso, all together on 'three.'" Any mainline pastor must be a specialist in hoisting dead weight.

As I move through my seventies, long after my "use by" date, victim of inevitable decay, I'm advantaged by God's having tutored me to put up with a broken-down body of Christ that, though always being resurrected, has broken legs, holes in the hands, and a nasty gash.

Jesus could have written a book, established an efficient system of public welfare, or founded an ethical improvement colloquium. Instead, gathering a group of ordinary people with a reckless and debonair "Follow me!," he did what he wanted done through them.

"Spirituality" is the rage these days—feeling religious, sort of, without the bother of people who are not as vaguely, agreeably spiritual. "Spirituality," the Jesus substitute at the moment, Jesus without a bride or a body, Jesus stripped of Euodia, Syntyche, Methodists, and me.

Though you think they would, no one withdraws from a congregation saying, "Jesus demands too much."

They leave muttering, "I think the world of Jesus; can't stand his friends."

Take my first congregation. Please. Rural Georgia (rural doesn't get more rural), I, fresh from Yale Divinity School, Bultmanned-Tilliched-and-Barthed-up for grad school at Emory. Saturday before my first Sunday I drove out to survey my assignment—misnamed Friendship Methodist Church. A large padlock hung from the front door. The lay leader—who laid carpet in Smyrna—explained that at a prayer meeting "people was ripping pews out of the floor, carting off memorial gifts they had give. So the sheriff come out and put on that there chain until the new preacher could come and talk some sense into them."

Standing in gray dust of the hot gravel parking lot, I thought, *I wanted to be William Sloane Coffin preaching to Christianity's cultured despisers, and the director of field work at Candler made me Margaret Mead stunned by the primitive puberty rites of Samoans.*

My days there were typified by squabbling, disappointment followed by undeniable failure, fornication between an alleged soprano and a bogus baritone after choir practice, Euodia and Syntyche duking it out in the parking lot before a wedding. When people asked, "Where is your church?" I replied, "Thirty miles and two centuries from Atlanta."

One day, in youthful despair, I poured out my frustration on a favorite Emory professor.

Dr. Hunter sympathetically listened—fisticuffs in the parking lot, choral cuckoldry. He agreed to the injustice of someone as talented as I forced to serve such losers as they.

"Worst of all," Hunter said, grinning, "Jesus says those whores and tax collectors get to go into the kingdom of God before us good people."

Church.

Though Karl Barth said that Christians go to church to make our last stand against God, I've seen enough of church to know that if I'm to be redeemed, it'll be along with Euodia and Syntyche, the Council of Bishops, What's-His-Name and his heavily made-up wife on TV from Houston, and the guy at Duke Chapel who judged my preaching "puerile," or not at all.

Jesus teaches, preaches, heals, suffers, and dies. Deserted by his own disciples, Christ enters paradise with nothing to show for his trouble but one slightly informed, barely penitent thief. Some trophy. And yet Barth says Jesus between two thieves on Calvary is the birthday of the church. Wherever Jesus is crucified in the company of criminals, there is the disarming way Jesus Christ has chosen to take back what belongs to him.

"Help these women," Paul implores, who have "laboured with me in the gospel," and who, for all their faults, are "my fellow-labourers, whose names are in the book of life." Even though they couldn't be ordained by the Presbyterian Church in America or the Southern Baptist Convention, these women are chosen by God to labor with Paul in the "work of the gospel." Called, they are under irrevocable orders to be reconciled. And Paul and I, as those called to lead, are under orders to work with them.

To whom did the resurrected Christ appear? Not to the cognoscenti *klēros* but to the squabbling *laos*—fearful, misunderstanding women who dared to preach resurrection to the disbelieving male disciples (Matt. 28:1–10). It's a heck of a way to run a kingdom of God, but it appears to be uniquely *his* way.

The New Testament loves the reciprocal pronoun "one another" (*allēlōn*). "Live in harmony with one another" (Rom. 12:16 ESV), admonish one another (Rom. 15:14), wait for one another (1 Cor. 11:33), build up one another (1 Thess. 5:11), submit to one another (Eph. 5:21), forgive one another (Col. 3:13), pray for one another (James 5:16). My personal favorite, "put up with one another" (Eph. 4:2 NIRV).

After a lecture in Chicago, Karl Barth was asked, "Do you think we'll see again those we love in heaven?" Barth, son of the church, replied, "Yes, I do. And those we hate."

The night I was ordained in 1973, at Broad Street Church in Clinton, when Bishop Tullis laid hands on my head, the Holy Spirit alighted upon me neither in the singing of the choir nor in the presence of adoring family and friends, but rather when the bishop intoned the ancient words of the Ordinal, "Never forget that the ones whom you serve are the beloved sheep of his fold for whom he died."

I knelt wondering, *Will the church appreciate my superior training and gifts? Might I have an all-electric parsonage? With how many Republicans must I do church?*

The Ordinal shook me: Don't forget, kid—the merely Methodist ones to whom you're lucky enough to preach to, to laugh and to weep with, to endure covered-dish suppers with, and to join in witnessing to the kingdom, are the ones for whom *he* died.

Just after Paul reasserts his calling as an apostle, he speaks of the baptismal calling of the whole church: "Paul, called to be an apostle of Jesus Christ. . . . For ye see your calling, . . . not many wise, . . . not many mighty, not many noble, are called: But God hath chosen the foolish things of the world to confound the wise;

. . . the weak things of the world to confound the . . . mighty; and base things of the world, and things which are despised, hath God chosen . . . to bring to nought things that are" (1 Cor. 1:1, 26–28).

We foolish, weak, base, and despised, we happy few, confounders of the mighty. *Church.*

*   *   *

Conned by Trinity's volunteer choir director, Peggy Hursey, into performing the delicate task of talking Victor out of singing in the choir—"Sweet man who is a helpless monotone," Peggy had said—I made Victor the head usher because, "Though you are doing a great job in the choir, as a salesman, you know how to welcome people."

"No need to lie to me. I was only singing in the choir because Peggy made me do it," said Victor. "Told her I couldn't sing."

Victor and Addie, both of them fifty and unmarried, met at the Arthur Murray dance class. He invited her to visit Trinity. In six months they danced their way to the altar for matrimony, making their vows before me and a packed church. Victor and Addie warned, "Some Sundays we won't be at church when we've got a dance contest across the state."

A year into marriage Addie was diagnosed with a debilitating nerve illness. This dance-loving newlywed was reduced to a bedridden paraplegic. Victor changed jobs in order to give Addie better care. The whole church grieved with them.

During one of my pastoral visits with Addie, she said to me, "Preacher, what do you think God wants me to do for my ministry now?"

Looking at her lying helpless in bed, I froze. "Er, uh, how do you mean?" I asked.

"Well, I can't do the things I did for the church before. Help me think what God wants me to do now," she said.

Lord, give me some help here.

I looked at the telephone that Victor had placed on her bed before he left for work. Under the guidance of the Holy Spirit, I said, "Well, er, as you know, Trinity is too small to have a church secretary. That means that I spend a lot of time on the phone. And we have a great need for keeping in touch with some of our convalescing members."

"Great idea! I'll be your telephone assistant," she exclaimed. "You just drop off a list of anybody who needs a call. I'll call them for you, then report at the end of the day."

I commissioned Addie as our telephone minister. Any person returning from a hospital stay got a daily call from Addie. All Sunday visitors were telephoned. Worshipers AWOL were called. People were reminded of meetings, recruited for church committees. Students were called after they left for college.

Morose Joe Brown reported for duty at the March trustee meeting. Disregarding our opening prayer, Joe began declaiming to the gathered trustees, "I come home from a helluva day at work. Dead tired. The big boss is in town tomorrow. So the wife says to me, 'Got a trustee meeting tonight at seven.' Just as I was saying I didn't have the strength to come to this meeting, that going out to this meeting could send a man in my condition to the grave, the phone rang. Addie's sweet voice said, 'Joe, we need you at the meeting tonight. Going to take a vote on the new roof. Can we count on you?'

"Now I ask you," he said, his voice rising, his gestures becoming more histrionic, "what sort of low, conniving, underhanded preacher would get a homebound, crippled, defenseless woman to shame a fellow Christian into coming to a church meeting? I ask you."

Church, I love you.

*   *   *

To everyone's surprise, there I was, 1998, delivering the final address at Robert Schuller's Crystal Cathedral Successful Church Conference. A thousand pastors had gathered around the theme "How to Succeed at Ministry." I, of course, chose "Failing at Ministry with Moses, Peter, and Just about Everybody in the Bible."

After my speech, an earnest young man approached, a pastor from the Dakotas. "Dr. Willimon," he said, "time and again, when I have thought of quitting, your words kept me here."

"Something *I* said?"

"Lutheran pastors' school in Fargo, you said, 'The church is a whore. Though you don't approve of how she makes money, she is your mother and you've got to find a way to love her anyway.'"

"Hey, kid, I didn't say that. Luther said it, more or less."

"I've got the tape," he threatened.

Just my luck to have that wisecrack chiseled on my tombstone.

Everyone who had heard me preach thought it odd that Robert Schuller would invite me to his sumptuous TV studio church that Sunday. I leapt at the invite; any publicity is better than none. One more opportunity to overcome my Southern inferiority, another merit badge for my sash. The Saturday before, Patsy and I were honored by Dr. and Mrs. Schuller in his private dining room (with matching china and monogrammed napkins) in the tower of the Crystal Cathedral.

Here's a snippet from the transcript of that interminable dinner:

Schuller said, "Like I said to Bill, 'Buddy, now we're going to find out just what you are made of. Character is proven in times like these.' Bill and Hillary, great folks."

I replied, "President and Mrs. Clinton? Actually, I have never met them."

"Really?" he said, attempting to get his mind around my shocking admission. "How often have you spoken at the White House?"

"Never. But I did do a walk-through with the Donaldson Elementary School Patrol Guards in 1958."

"Remarkable." He said it as if I'd just told him I was still a virgin. "I've been the confidant of every president since Dick. Actually, I find the term 'sermon' woefully archaic. I haven't preached a 'sermon' in thirty years. I share 'messages.' 'Sermon' is a turnoff for folks in California. Surely that's true even where you're from. 'Sharing' is more culturally sensitive than 'preaching.' Coretta still honors the term 'sermon,' and, goodness knows, her husband was a master."

Coretta Scott King?

"Say, you've preached at the National Cathedral?" he persisted.

"Once," I admitted glumly.

"Once? You must do more to get your name before the public. Media is everything. What's the size of your congregation at Duke?"

"Oh, on a good Sunday, as many as seventeen hundred." I was unable to cover my humiliation. "Most Sundays, fewer, I guess."

"Goodness gracious! Why cover your light under a bushel? TV sways the world. Tomorrow, in the Cathedral, you will speak to ten million! But tell me, how were you selected one of the Twelve Most Effective Preachers in the English Speaking World?"

"Uh, that was done by a couple of Baylor profs. They surveyed a bunch of preachers, I believe."

"Odd," said my host, eyes like steely drills. "I'm sure you were embarrassed by such a strange designation. What were their criteria for judgment? Doesn't sound scientific. Well, it has certainly enhanced your reputation, that is, among a certain audience. More surprising, why have you not invited *me* to preach at Duke Chapel?" he asked.

"Er, uh, like, that would be wonderful. Are you open to our invitation?"

"Perhaps. You would need to talk to my agent," he said, swishing around the ice in his glass. "I would do what I could to adjust the honorarium, though I'm booked solid through 2005."

And if Jesus returns in 1999?

"I'm in Honolulu this Sunday. Won't see you preach, though millions will!" Schuller laughed heartily, sure I would screw up. "My pilots can get us there by the time of the organ prelude with the dancing fountains. Well, I've enjoyed hearing about your honors and all. But don't want to keep you out too late. With all the heightened expectation—you being one of the Twelve Most Effective Preachers in the English Speaking World—you must be on top of your game. Our pulpit has welcomed the most gifted communicators in the world, not just the 'English-speaking world'" (air quotes made with hands). "We're hoping to get Magic Johnson in the fall. Larry King was just here. Makeup, seven sharp."

I'd love to have you on the Donaldson Elementary School ground at recess when the teacher wasn't looking.

The next morning, the makeup artist said, "Honey, let's do something about those splotches. Everything shows on TV."

"I've got worse flaws."

"Hi, Will. I'm Sherry, your producer," called a cutesy voice.

Producer?

"My job is to make your message all that it can be. Just a reminder, try to keep up your tempo. Look right into that camera and sell it to the folks at home. Make us want it! Our surveys show that they just eat up sincerity."

"I'll try to act sincere," I said, through layers of makeup and hair spray.

"That's the spirit! Is this your first time?"

First time?

"Oh, I've preached on TV lots of times," I lied.

"Good! So I don't have to worry about your getting all nervous, even if you will be speaking to millions," said Sherry, my producer. "Nerves work against your looking sincere. Okay?"

"Sincerity is my goal."

Greased up and oozing sincerity, I entered the pulpit as the organ rumbled and the fountains gushed in homage to Freud. Patsy, seated next to a UCLA law student I had taught as an undergrad, heard Mark marvel, "Will looks like a corpse! Or a badly painted drag queen."

After my first couple of sentences, I glanced over my left shoulder and was stunned by a gigantic image of myself, crooked teeth and all, on the huge screen behind me.

Damn the Greenville dentist who dismissed my mother's request to straighten my teeth with "Why? He's not a girl!"

After the first service, my producer, Sherry, came in, headphones ajar. "Way to go, William! Nice. On this next take at eleven I want you to really make us want it."

It?

"Sell it! Keep your rhythm going, give us all you've got, keep up the tempo all the way to the end. Don't peak too soon. OK?"

My mother doesn't allow me to engage in this sort of conversation.

"And I need you, this time, to begin your sermon by thanking your good friend Dr. Schuller for inviting you," said Sherry, my producer. "Give me about a forty-five to the right, extend your hand as you thank Dr. Schuller. We'll paste Dr. Schuller in for the broadcast. And of course, give us a great big smile. Don't worry about your teeth."

I don't belong in Southern California.

"The Hour of Power," my three hours of glower.

As a liveried chauffeur grimly held open the limousine door, eager to deposit me at the airport, a disheveled man came up to the sedan calling, "Preacher! Preacher! Great message, what I could understand of it through your accent. Must be an incredible experience to speak from Dr. Schuller's pulpit. How did Dr. Schuller hear about you?"

I dove into the limo. The man ran alongside, shouting, "I hated church. Didn't know which way to turn. I'm one of the thousands Dr. Schuller has saved. This is church like it's meant to be."

When I returned to Duke Chapel, my assistant, Jackie Andrews, asked, "What's Dr. Schuller really like? I'm sure there's more than what we see on TV."

"No, there isn't," I replied, in love. "I'll say this: In a three-hour dinner with that braggart, I couldn't get a word in."

Hardly looking up from her keyboard, Jackie marveled, "His ego is bigger than *yours*?"

∗   ∗   ∗

The Church of the Reconciler in Birmingham serves breakfast to over a hundred homeless people every morning. Visits to Church of the Rec were analgesic for my depression due to the state of the UMC. One morning I noticed a man in the kitchen washing dishes, up to his elbows in dishwater. (The pastor believes that the homeless ought to be served on china rather than plastic.) I recognized him, a high-powered lawyer, member of our largest, most affluent suburban congregation.

"It's wonderful that you are here, washing dishes for the homeless," I complimented him.

"Good," he mumbled, not looking up from his work.

"Have you always enjoyed ministry with the homeless?" I persisted.

"Who told you I enjoyed working with the homeless? Have you met the homeless? Most of 'em are so crazy or addicted that nobody wants 'em home."

"Well, er, uh, that makes it all the more remarkable what you are doing," I said. "How did you get here?"

He looked up from the dishwater and replied with aggravation, "*Jesus* put me here. How did *you* get here? You really wanted to be bishop of Birmingham?"

Church.

*   *   *

On the Sunday after the presidential election debacle, I preached in a United Methodist church in the suburbs of Washington, DC. The pastor had told me that he expected to lose as many as thirty families—Obama political appointees sure to be purged. My text was the assigned epistle for the day, Romans 5, "Christ died for the ungodly." I reminded the faithful that gracious Jesus died for sinners, only sinners, and that Jesus got into all manner of trouble eating and drinking with tax collectors and whores.

My sermon concluded with "OK, good for us. We have elected a lying, adulterous, draft-evading, bankruptcy-declaring, misogynistic, racist riverboat gambler with tacky gold plumbing fixtures. He is a national disgrace *and*" (pause for effect) "*one whom Jesus Christ loves, saves, and for whom he gave his life.*" (Leaning over the pulpit, looking into the whites of their eyes) "*Are you sure that you want to worship that much of a Savior?*"

At the church door with the host pastor, postsermon, bracing for the ire of disgruntled Methodists, words sounded in my brain: *A Methodist preacher is all you'll ever be.*

5

Unplanned Disruptions

Saul, yet breathing out threatenings and slaughter against the disciples of the Lord, went unto the high priest, and desired of him letters to Damascus to the synagogues, that if he found any of this way, whether they were men or women, he might bring them bound unto Jerusalem. And as he journeyed, . . . suddenly there shined round about him a light from heaven: And he fell to the earth, and heard a voice saying unto him, Saul, Saul, why persecutest thou me? And he said, Who art thou, Lord? And the Lord said, I am Jesus whom thou persecutest. . . . And there was a certain disciple at Damascus, named Ananias; and to him said the Lord in a vision, Ananias. And he said, Behold, I am here, Lord. And the Lord said unto him, Arise, and go into the street which is called Straight, and inquire . . . for one called Saul, of Tarsus. . . . Ananias answered, Lord, I have heard by many of this man, how much evil he hath done to thy saints. . . . But the Lord said unto him, Go thy way: for he is a chosen vessel unto me, to bear my name before the Gentiles, and kings, and the children of Israel: For I will shew him how great things he must suffer for my name's sake. (Acts 9:1–16)

When I presided at Tom Wolfe's burial in Richmond, I recalled our first meeting. Showing off the facade of our chapel to Tom, I noted Duke's curious collection of welcoming "saints"—Thomas Jefferson (Deist), Robert E. Lee (recently removed, but Tom, a graduate of Washington and Lee, had thought that his presence on the front of a church made perfect sense), and Sydney Lanier (unknown to anybody but Tom). The prominent display of these Southerners on a campus church was what you got when Duke's first president was an English professor (born near Greenville, an 1889 graduate of Wofford).

On the left side of the porch we are greeted by famous preachers (of course).

"All were carved by Italians that Duke brought to Durham after they had built Princeton," I said.

"I'd guess that's Saint Francis," said Tom.

"Good guess, but no, that's a Dominican, Savonarola," I lectured. "Florentine troublemaker."

"You must be kidding," said Tom, taking a step back in white-suited wonderment. "Only the church would pull a stunt like that."

It was late that night before I recalled Tom's blockbuster *Bonfire of the Vanities*. In blazing sermons Savonarola urged rich Florentines to throw their finery upon his bonfire rather than to allow their riches to drag them into hell. Eventually the Medici had a bellyful of this hellfire preaching and roasted the preacher.

"Welcome to church, all you upwardly mobile Dukies," says Savonarola at the left of the chapel's front door. "After service, join me at the bonfire, where we'll toss your MBAs, keys to the Porsche, birth-control devices, and other assorted trifles in the flames." Only the church would pull a stunt like that.

It's odd that some characterize God's creative work as the making of order and stability. I've found the opposite to be true; you'll know it's the Trinity if it's disruptive. Because of God's refusal to leave well enough alone, Christians' lives are always on the verge of being out of control. Jesus intrudes among us not to care but to call. Disciples are made, not born. Jeremiah compared God's ways with Israel to a potter pounding a lump of clay to make something out of a mess of mud (Jer. 18:1–12). Disruption—conversion, *metanoia*, relinquishment, detoxification, purgation, renovation—characterizes the work of the divine potter who pounded Abraham, Mary, Paul, and maybe me. There are bound to be bonfires.

Barth taught me that when interpreting an odd biblical text, mind the gap between you and God. The question to put to a passage of Scripture is not the modern, self-important, "How is this relevant to my life?" or, "How can I make this text make sense?" The proper question, said Barth, is, "How is God calling me to change? What would I have to relinquish, for this text to make sense?"

Scripture's sly intent is not agreement but conversion. Something is gained, yes, but much can be lost as well. After

a service, an attendee says, "You preachers never talk about anything that's related to my world."

I try to find a nice way to say, "Idiot! Scripture doesn't want to 'relate to your world.' Scripture rocks your world."

Watching a Duke quarterback wolf down a near lethal amount of steak at the lunch I paid for, I asked, "Well, what do you think of what we do on Sundays at Duke Chapel?"

"I don't think about it," he responded with his mouth full. "Never been in the chapel."

"You've been a student here for three years and have never attended a service at the chapel?" I said, pushing my chair back from the table. "God, give me patience!"

"Never felt the need. I went to church some when I was a kid. From what I can remember, Christians are always trying to get people to change, to be better people. I'm happy with my life the way it is right now, so I don't see the need. Are you going to eat those fries?"

"That's a surprisingly intelligent reason not to come to church," I marveled. "I shall do that in needlepoint, frame it, and put it over the chapel's front door, just under the statue of John Wesley, across from Savonarola—*Achtung!* God at work. Dare not enter this chapel if you're risk averse to emerging as a different person."

A young plumber once timidly told me that Jesus had appeared to him one night as he was coming home late from work. "As real as you please. There he was. Standing in front of me, on my back porch, like he had been waiting, like he needed me for something."

When I asked why he had never told anyone about the epiphany, he replied, "If what I saw was really real, if Jesus is true, then I couldn't keep being the same as I am. I love my wife and family, so I couldn't afford to admit it was Jesus."

Or, as Jürgen Moltmann put it, people disbelieve in the bodily resurrection of Jesus because, if it were true, their lives would look ridiculously out of step.

*   *   *

In calling disciples, disruptive Jesus was a notorious home wrecker. Nobody follows Jesus without, to some degree, disobeying the fifth commandment. In my years as dean of the chapel, I had maybe twenty anxious phone calls: "Help! I sent my child to Duke to be a success, and she has become a religious fanatic!"

"Religious fanatic" defined as, rather than law school, running away with the Catholics to a literacy program in Haiti.

"Hey, lady, I'm from Greenville, home of Bob Jones University. Catholics in Haiti ain't fanaticism." These parents may be ignorant of the specifics of the Christian faith, may have never heard of Savonarola, but at least they know to tremble at the first whiff of the bonfires of Jesus.

In an age of anxious parents constantly sizing up their children, then lamenting, "What did we do wrong?," we're surprised that the Bible tells us nothing about the families of Israel's prophets. Paul briefly goes autobiographical to highlight that he didn't have a life worth mentioning until Jesus fanaticized him on the Damascus road. Only Luke reports the single episode from Jesus's childhood (2:41–52)—Mary and Joseph's abandonment of little Jesus at the temple (for *two days*, no hovering parents, they). Scripture's lack of interest in childhood, parents, and family is born of the conviction that God is more responsible for you than Mom or Dad.

Inappropriate weening, abusive peers in high school, or parental ineptitude can't force anybody to be other than who God wants them to be. In two decades of campus ministry, I played Savonarola, pursuing students into bars, dorms, even among the tents at the Krzyzewskiville basketball-ticket campout, as I badgered, "What's God done with you lately?" Thereby I had a front-row seat to watch God weasel into the university, shake up an unsuspecting adolescent life, casting it beyond the reach of imperial parents. I saw firsthand Flannery O'Connor's "action of grace in territory held largely by the devil."

Socrates was executed as a "corrupter of the young"; the only thing Socrates and Jesus shared was a low opinion of the prerogatives of parents.

In ornithology, an "accident" is a "vagrant," a bird outside of its range. At the university I was a vagrant attempting to steady my perch on a power line with birds not of my feather, forced by God, whether I wanted or not, to be an evangelist and missionary, wolf in Methodist guise, God's mole who tells the university the open secret that Jesus Christ died for purposes even more noble than diversity, deconstruction, gender self-assignment, the Office of Institutional Equity, ACC basketball, or safe sex.

I received a summons to a confab with the dean of students. "We're preparing to install machines—with a public health symbol, tastefully done—in all the restrooms at Duke," said a subdean.

"Men's and women's," chimed another. "Even the library."

The library! I knew they weren't in there reading.

"As Director of Religious Life, how do you think religious people will receive this bold initiative?"

Responding on behalf of all religious types, I said, "Where were you guys when I was in college and needed you? I'm a Methodist. You'll never get moral pushback from us, though I wish. But the Catholics won't take this sitting down, or lying down, or however they take it."

"The Catholic Church has its head in the sand," exclaimed an assistant to the assistant dean, a postpapist.

Then the Holy Spirit put words in my mouth: "Speaking for all religious people, we're in favor of these machines only if they're like the ones in cheap gas station men's rooms. You know, with the naked woman on a fake leopard skin rug."

"You're not serious," said a dean's valet.

"That way we can make our point: 'Boys and girls, sex is good. God created it, Genesis 1:27. But it's not worth killing somebody. So use these condoms. On the other hand, if you would like to grow up to be the sort of person who doesn't rut until you've first learned someone's name, come on over to the chapel. We'll shake you up and teach you how to get back at your parents.'"

That day I rejoiced with David before Goliath: the Lord hath delivered mine enemies into my hand (1 Sam. 17:46).

*   *   *

Peter Gomes, Harvard's late, great preacher and my still-lamented friend, used to say to me over his extrasweet old-fashioned, on the eve of Peter's annual outburst from the chapel pulpit, "Friend, you and I are dinosaurs, doomed for extinction, unable to reproduce ourselves. The university church has had its day. *Après nous le déluge.*"

Another sip. "Students threaten clergy less theologically confident than you and I. Chapels that once had the guts to utter the disruptive 'J Word' to the young will dwindle to tiny gatherings of ancient, groveling Unitarians and gawking tourists."

Peter and I, mainline Protestant hegemony's last collegiate hurrah. In our day, nobody better worked what's left of Christendom. The morbidity of university chapels is particularly sad because students live at that rare confluence when a stage in human development aligns with the inclinations of the Trinity. Whereas most grown-ups spend our energies consolidating the life we've got, young adults love surprises, enjoy being born again, and then again, paying ridiculously high tuition for the privilege of striding in and daring the faculty, "Hit me! Give me your best shot! Make me somebody more worthwhile than I would have been had I not come to college!"

*   *   *

Billy Graham accepted my invitation to preach in Duke Chapel. To my surprise, Billy is the nicest evangelical famous preacher one could hope to meet—unlike a TV preacher in Houston I'm too charitable to mention. Billy was so admired by so many for so long because Billy never stopped preaching God's disruptive gift of a second chance. One of Billy's best-selling books was *How to Be Born Again.*

His sermon in Duke Chapel was a muddle—set pieces from Billy's work over the years, lots of Bible thrusting but with little biblical content, and devoid of any discernible theme. Nobody noticed. Just being among the crowd as Billy preaches is sermon enough.

We mainline, nonevangelical, noninvasive preachers pat a congregation on the head as we murmur, "There, there, God loves you as you are. Promise me you won't change a thing." Billy consistently preached the gospel of the second chance. Those in desperate need of a second or third chance require more than "progressive" sermons—Jesus just hanging with people as they are, bourgeois conformity with a spiritual tint, offering a bit of a spiritual nudge. Buttoned-down mainline Christianity offers aspirin for those in need of massive chemotherapy.

"You will have a wonderful ministry here," Billy reassured me as we stood in my study after service. "Many of these students and faculty are unaware that Christ is eager to have them."

I'm sorry that Karl Barth disapproved of Billy's preaching. And I wish Billy had not been cynically snookered by Nixon. Sometimes we evangelists, in an effort to love someone for Christ, get seduced. In reaching out to speak to the world, we fall in facedown. Tricky Dick and I need all the second chances God's got. Shortly after Billy's sermon in Duke Chapel, Margie Velma Barfield fed her North Carolina preacher husband tapioca laced with ant poison, thus provoking his gut-wrenching death. When the state medical examiner suspected foul play, the man's body was dug up. The sheriff supervising the exhumation was asked if an autopsy would confirm murder. "All I know is that there ain't a damn ant in a mile of this here cemetery."

Velma, who probably murdered many, some by arsenic, others by arson, was easily convicted and ordered to be executed. While I organized protests, Billy's helpmate, Ruth Bell Graham, corresponded with Velma on death row. Velma took the Graham cure, repented, asked Christ into her heart, and was redeemed. Ruth and I pled with the (liberal Presbyterian) governor to spare Velma. Governor Hunt—committed more to equal rights for women than to the disruptive God of the Second Chance—refused, making Velma the first woman to be executed in North Carolina in decades.

Back when I served as junior high rep to the Official Board of Buncombe Street Church, Billy announced a citywide crusade in Greenville. The whole town mobilized. At the board meeting, grown-ups debated our congregation's participation.

"Bunch of Baptists trying to get a leg up on us," gasped one.

"Graham says that there will be no separation of the races during the meetings." That did it. The board voted to protect our church from Grahamesque miscegenation and refused participation.

After the meeting, as I exited a side door to catch the segregated Greenville bus to go home, down a dark church hallway I heard weeping. I crept down the hall. Light shown from an open door. I peeked in. Our pastor, Dr. Dubose, was sobbing, holding his head in his hands. Keeping up with the disruptive movements of a righteous God is not for the faint of heart.

When I saw our pastor weeping, my first thought was not *That's sad*, but rather *I'm going to date his daughter.* Still, I thank God that at an early age I got to see what makes preachers cry.

*   *   *

My Damascus road divine disruption, though incomparable to Velma's, occurred when I was sixteen. (Christ loves to accost defenseless youth but seems to lose active interest in seniors.) You already know that I grew up in an unashamedly, legally white-supremacist culture. Each day I boarded a Greenville bus that bore the sign: *South Carolina Law: White patrons sit from the front. Colored patrons sit from the rear.* Nobody questioned that sign, especially those who preached to me on Sunday.

My church sent me to a youth conference at Lake Junaluska, beloved (alcohol-free, smoke-free, and lust-free) Methodist resort in the mountains of North Carolina.

At registration, a grown-up whispered, "We hear that you are a nice boy."

Obviously the lady had not heard about the intermission of the junior/senior prom.

"Are you willing to room with a Neeeegro?" Ever eager to burnish my positive self-image, I said, "Yes." I was assigned a room with another sixteen-year-old from Greenville. When I walked in, there he sat on the opposite bed, better prepared for me than I was for him. We were strangers, even though his Methodist church was less than a mile from Buncombe Street; he went to a school four blocks from Greenville High and played on ball fields where we never ventured.

I recall nothing of what was said from the podium that weekend, but I'll never forget our conversation that lasted until dawn Saturday night. Charles told me what it was like to worship at John Wesley rather than Buncombe Street. He described in detail attending a school worlds away from mine, and asked me about life at my school, from which he was legally excluded. To paraphrase Langston Hughes, my Greenville was never Greenville to him.

"Does it bother you that there are laws that separate us, keep you in your place and me in mine?" he asked.

"I guess I never thought about it."

"Don't you see? They want to trap both of us."

By sunrise, I had my world skillfully cracked open, exposed, infinitely expanded, disrupted, ministered to by another who—like Ananias for Saul, Marney for me, Ruth for Velma—was kind enough to take me where I couldn't have gone without help. I once was blind but now I see. I left Lake Junaluska better than I had been bred to be.

Before heading back to our separate worlds, Charles confessed, "When I saw that the church had forced me to room with a white guy, I was scared shitless."

The risen Christ egging on Charles, even at sixteen, for risky, faithful, color-courageous witness in service to my conversion. Even as Ananias was enlisted by God to open the eyes of Church Enemy Number One, so Charles was summoned to cure the blindness of Christ Enemy Number One, *me*.

Only the church would pull a stunt like that, forcing me to room with my enemy who might also be my savior coaching me through disruptive second birth. Years later I heard Garry Wills say that if you are a male white Southerner over fifty—(guilty)—there is no way to convince you that people can't change. You have experienced such seismic shifts and radical reformation in your own heart, in your family, and in your world that you believe God is able.

Natural law is a fiction devised to help us cope with our contingency before God. Sorry, anal-retentive legalists, the world was not created by a lawyer. Orderliness is not God's chief attribute; the future is whatever Jesus means it to be, whether you cooperate or not. There will be surprises.

"How can my daughter, a PhD physicist, be expected to believe in the bodily resurrection of Jesus?" asked errant Bishop Spong during a debate.

"It all depends," I responded, "on her tolerance for disruption. We've all known limited physicists. Does she enjoy surprises? Has she ever traveled outside of New Jersey?"

"No accident is in God," said Thomas Aquinas. Nothing about God is accidental, added, needing modification or perfection. God exists in perfection. If everything about God is essential, not accidental, this implies that almost everything about us humans is accidental, awaiting further fabrication by God.

Aquinas employed Aristotelian concepts of substance and accident in his theology of eucharistic transubstantiation: the accidents of appearance and taste of bread and wine don't change, but the substance changes to the Body and Blood. *Substance* is what's most real; *accidents* are not of the essence of a thing. Though this sort of body/soul bifurcation of the Eucharist sent Protestants spinning, it was Thomas's way of denoting the divinity of the Eucharist. Only God is essential; we're accidental all the way down.

Some modern philosophers turned Aristotle's thought on accidents and substance on its head. Harvard's W. V. O. Quine argued that there's no such thing as "essential properties" in humans or the world; every property is an accident, ascribed, denoted. Essentialist accounts of the self are too static, fail to account for differences in selves, and act as if God's work in us is done at our conception. *Nein.* Jeremiah was just another fetus until God's vocation made him a disruptive prophet.

All this philosophizing means that it's impossible to separate my accidental vocation from the essential me. God's external, added call makes me thoroughly me. What seems to me an accident is, through the eyes of faith, Providence. You'll never hear me say, "I happen to be from Greenville, South Carolina," or "I happened to attend Wofford College," much less, "It was just my luck to be a writer."

I believe that most of the good that happens to us is accidental, in the philosophical sense of the word. In psychology, "attribution theory" has shown that we tend to attribute positive events to interior factors (my good intentions, my charitable disposition, or my hard work). We blame negative events upon exterior factors (the slights and injustices I've suffered at the hands of other people, lousy luck, absentee father). The gospel turns attribution theory on its head. People who dare to assert that it's "God who has made us and not we ourselves" believe that any good that we have thought or done is attributable to an exterior (i.e., God) factor.

Paul Tillich's sentimental sermon urging "accept your acceptance" (who doesn't love that advice when you are raising hell in college?) is an injustice to the discombobulating, topsy-turvy bloody love of Jesus that gives lives worth leading and deaths worth dying by offering us more than if left to our own devices. Jesus has grander designs than blasé "unconditional love."

*   *   *

Much systematic theology attempts to stabilize a restlessly converting God who thinks nothing of putting people like me in vocational pain. Around the divinity school, novice clergy are urged to "keep Sabbath" because clergy are so zealously committed to helping others that the incessantly nagging laity compel us to be overweight, overstressed, and underpaid. The ten-million-dollar Duke Clergy Health study claims empirically to have proved as much.

I'm all for leisure, a day off, a round of golf, or whatever helps one endure the rigors of working for the Lord. But much of this talk about the beauty of Sabbath keeping (except that of my buddy Walt Brueggemann), candle lighting, centering, self-care, deep breathing, and anxiety reduction sounds suspiciously like an attempt to give theological justification for bourgeois efforts to tame a living, demanding God. Privileged, powerful people enjoy thinking of ourselves as terribly overworked. When you are on top, capable, committed, having to run the world all by yourself, so deeply sensitive to other people's pain, it leads to fatigue, doesn't it?

Even less defensible is talk about the need for clergy to attain a good "life-work balance." Balance is the atheistic delusion that your life is under your control. Hands laid upon pastors' heads give us lives less important than our work and render us unable neatly to separate "life" from "work." Vocation throws off balance the modern, essentialist, narcissistic myth that we are most truly ourselves when we de-role, stripping ourselves of commitments and responsibility for anyone but ourselves.

Jesus was a well-documented Sabbath breaker. "Centering" (only dead animals are found in the middle of the road), "life-work balance" (nobody accused Jesus of that), "self-care" (sounds like something you didn't want your mother to catch you doing) fail to do justice to the peculiarity of the called-for life.

A misguided group at our school proposed that once a student had put in fifteen hours a week for a class, the student was done. "What do you think this is, the Law School?" I ridiculed. If pastors lack the skill to produce a sermon in fifteen hours, they push on, wondering why God called someone as limited as they to preach. We work longer hours in faith that God hasn't made a mistake in calling us, of all people, to care for God's people. The work is more sacred than the stable mental health of the worker.

Ingratiating preachers transform Jesus's cross into a snuggly bourgeois blanket. I was recently subjected to a sermon at Yale Divinity School on Matthew 13:1–5, the prelude to the parable of the sower, in which the preacher cited "Jesus sat down" to urge seminarians to stop busily studying, to carve out time to follow Jesus's example and courageously *sit*.

Pastors who feel oppressed by the duties of ministry ought to consider if, one, they are so unskilled in the arts of leadership that they make God look bad by implying that faithful ministry is impossible, or, two, they lack the gifts and the call by God to be a pastor. If my doctor began my consultation by complaining of cloying patients and the unbearable stress of her job, I would have my prostate exam elsewhere.

"You'll never hear me complain about how hard I'm working," said one of my students a year into pastoral ministry. "Young adult male unemployment in this county is over 30 percent. I've got church folks who would give anything for a stressful job." Thanks, Jesus and the bishop, for forcing clerics into situations that chasten our clericalism.

When the dean menacingly hinted, "Isn't it time that you thought about retirement?" I replied, "Why? I'm already a professor, the closest one can come to full-time leisure without having to endure a retirement dinner." My model is Calvin, who, at his end, asked to be propped on pillows and a book placed in his weak hands. "Would you have God come and find me idle?"

*　　　*　　　*

Paul wasn't searching for a more fulfilling life; he was hunting down wackos from The Way. God was searching for him. Paul has a story worth retelling because God rewrote the story of Saul. A missionary to the gentiles is all Paul will ever be.

Christ then called Ananias to tell Saul—Church Enemy Number One—that he was going to knock him off balance and require him to suffer as never before for handing over the good news. And if those life trajectories make life tough for Paul and Ananias, God doesn't care.

Later, Paul said that after God took him up to the third heaven (wherever that is), the Lord gave him a "thorn in the flesh" (whatever that was). *The Lord gave? After God's blessing, God's affliction?* I ask as I nervously count my surfeit of blessings.

Even after his dramatic throw-down by the risen Christ, Paul had to keep growing and submit to instruction (Acts 9:19). As Barth said, in the Christian faith one is always an amateur, never so adept at the faith that one need not admit, "I got that wrong," turn and become as a little child, and submit to rebirth.

Among my continuing conversions are these: from thinking that Socrates was a hero, that liberalism and Christianity can sleep together, that racism is found solely in South Carolina, that the university is a place of intellectual passion, that Dickens and D. H. Lawrence are great writers, that politics is the best way to change the world, that Reinhold Niebuhr is a theologian, that Raphael is saccharine, that revelation flows from the top (clergy) down (laity), and that I'm too smart to be a Methodist.

Assembling the creatively titled *Collected Sermons of William H. Willimon*, I had the painful experience of having my nose rubbed in decades of my sermons. Though I'd like to think that I've always been me, from the first, I haven't. Surprise, God corrected me along the way, just what you'd expect of an out-of-control God who would blind a Pharisee midlife in order for him, at the end, to see Light.

In *Grace Abounding to the Chief of Sinners*, incarcerated John Bunyan gave birth to autobiography as narration of purgation. Bunyan said that he could have gone on at greater length about his "temptations and troubles for sin," but to do so might dishonor God and even flatter Satan. Sorry to rebuff your prurient curiosity; my peccadillos, being chiefly vocational rather than sexual or financial, little compliment Satan.

As a young pastor, I was warned by sexist pastors, beware the temptresses who lurk in the congregation.

"I came to her home, midmorning, to offer pastoral care after the death of her husband," the pastor alleged, "and she lunged at me in this pink, fluffy see-through negligee. Son, be careful."

These male clergy narratives have all the veracity of a Saturday night Pi Kappa Alpha postparty brag session. In four decades of ministry, nothing like this has ever happened to me. And I'm an attractive male. Right?

One of my anxieties about the episcopacy was having to discipline clergy who violated professional boundaries. I always interviewed the victim, if she was willing. After listening to a person who had come to the church in her time of need, only to have some sleazy clergyman take advantage of her vulnerability, I found it easy to say to the perpetrator, "It has been my good fortune to be called to be a Methodist preacher. Someone like you discredits an otherwise great vocation. Good-bye."

Years ago, I prepared to write on clergy ethics by reading the church fathers' thought on ministry. The patriarchs feared the lure of money more than a misused negligee. (Did you know that "negligee" is from the French, "neglected"? I'm giving you that for free.)

At my very first annual conference, a well-meaning older pastor took me aside, "Boy, here's advice I wish someone had given me: Buy property at Junaluska."

Three agonizing years of Greek for this?

"Every man on the cabinet owns a cottage at Junaluska. It's the key to success in this conference. At least a condominium."

Mama, if that's movin' up, I'm movin' out.

As my church dithers over whether or not to ordain on the basis of how a person has coitus, I remind them that two out of three of Satan's temptations of Jesus (Matt. 4:1–11) were material rather than spiritual. None was sexual.

Patsy has helped me overcome some of my inbred acquisitiveness. I give thanks that Patsy is so congenitally well formed in Wesleyanism that she insisted, even in our early impoverishment, that we tithe. We took a pay cut with every move, including our move to the episcopacy. When unexpected higher salaries came our way, Patsy urged 20 percent. Today we thwart the IRS by giving the majority of our income to church, school, and mission. If wee scoundrel Zacchaeus can open his coffers as material certification of his conversion, so can we (Luke 19:8). Our attempts to manage money like Christians have endowed scholarships at half a dozen institutions and made us partners with scores of ministries.

I doubt our tithe impresses Jesus (Luke 18:9–14), and to be honest, we've gotten more than we have given. Still, acts of financial supererogation have helped us chip away at our natural propensity toward materialism. Money and self-deceit are bed-

fellows. Giving has helped us to stare American Mammon in the face and sneer, "Oh great Gog and Magog, two-thirds of us is still God's."

Looking over our tax return, I hear Augustine preach that "a rich man is either a thief or the son of a thief." Ouch. Of all the people Jesus called to "Follow me!," only one refused—his rebuff of discipleship was due to money (Matt. 19:16–30).

Fledgling preachers, I tell my seminarians, must decide up front how much money they require in order to preach the gospel without resentment toward Jesus. "More good sermons have been deflated by the prospect of a five hundred dollar raise than by fear of an inquisition," said my preaching prof. As John Wesley told early Methodists, little talent is required to get money; look who's got it. It's a sign of a full dose of the Holy Spirit when the greedy become generous, or words to that effect.

*   *   *

By sprinkling water on my head in my grandmother's living room after a big Sunday dinner, did that overfed, underpaid country preacher intend to throw me into the arms of a disruptive, demanding God? In what way was my baptism also a bonfire of my vanities? Did my gathered, extended family that afternoon realize that Jesus loves to rescue Willimons from the clutches of family in order to bind them to his odd family called church? I doubt it.

Thank God that whether the baptizers knew or didn't know, the church knows (ever since the Donatist controversy): the baptizer's intentions, understandings, or deficiencies are not the point. God will get what God wants.

I'm a better person because I was baptized and ordained. Sometimes I look at seminary students and wonder if that's an appeal of pastoral ministry. They are (just like me), by nature and upbringing, cowardly, lustful, weak, materialistic, and deceitful and are therefore (like me) attracted to a profession that promises to convert them, to make them better than they would be if Jesus had left them alone.

"Just be with people," unctuous pastoral care professors simper. "Don't try to fix or change them. That's arrogant and insensitive. Simply be with them in affirming, incarnational presence." The upper middle class has a myriad of ways to tame the Holy Spirit. Those who drive cars like mine tend to be threatened by the notion that God has a more important project than our emotional well-being and stability. I thank God that on a night at Lake Junaluska, Charles had enough faith to believe God could renovate even a white boy like me.

I'm not sure I've tried to "fix" church members in trouble, but I hope I had the guts to help them figure out how, even in their pain, God was calling them. The same God who demands a witness even from someone who is homeless or from the person who has stage four cancer certainly demands privileged persons like us to do our bit in the war.

Most people in my income tax bracket have the good sense to know that if unbalanced, non-Sabbatarian, disruptive, out-of-control Jesus grabbed hold of us, enlisted us, and summoned us to care for something more important than a good "life-work balance," our lives would become more unmanageable. Better to just be with people and bless the status quo as the extent of Jesus's work.

From what I saw as bishop, clergy's greatest challenge is productivity rather than a good life-work balance. At its best, Methodism has believed that God calls clergy not to an office, a status, but to lend a hand in God's work through God's people in God's world. In the Gospel of John Jesus says he is the light of the world (John 8:12). More astounding, in Matthew, Jesus looks upon his ragtag followers and says, "*You* are the light of the world. Shine!" (Matt. 5:14, paraphrased).

Just as it is a theological mistake for mainline liberals to weight incarnation more than redemption, grave damage has been done in evangelical Protestantism by detaching salvation from vocation, misleading people into thinking that God's intentions are only to save them without deploying them. After Paul on the Damascus road, everyone who claims "I have taken Jesus into my heart" ought to be asked, "So where is Jesus now taking you?"

Patsy and I were meeting with one of our Spanish-speaking congregations near Birmingham. Through a translator I asked them to share some highlight from their ministry.

"Last Sunday was good," said one of the lay leaders. Widespread agreement in the group.

"We came to the time for prayer requests. Alicia asked for prayers for her next-door neighbor whose husband beat her. Alicia said she heard the husband shouting when she left for church that morning. That's when Pastor said, 'We don't need to ask Jesus to bother with this. Come on, let's go!' Pastor led us all out of the church and into the parking lot. We all got into cars, except for the kids."

"Wow," said I.

"We went to Alicia's apartment house. We got out. Pastor banged on the man's door. 'Open up in the name of Jesus!' he shouted. The man cursed us and told us to go away. Pastor knocked again. Then José and Raul kicked down the door. Pastor warned the man not to stand in our way when we were working for Jesus. We got the poor woman and her two children. We told them we would look after them and they would be safe with us."

"Wow."

"Pastor told the husband what he needed to do if he ever wanted to see his wife and children again. He rebuked the unclean spirit. Then we all came back to church and finished the service. After lunch, we filed a report with the police. Pastor has visited the man in jail and thinks we have a chance with him."

"Wow"—the most this merchant of words could muster.

(BTW: That disruptively vibrant Christian congregation was destroyed in one night, vaporized, after Alabama Republicans passed their anti-immigration bill that was so mean-spirited that Duke alumnus Stephen Miller had to write the legislation for them.)

*   *   *

It is my good fortune to be deposited by Christ, by vocation, in a more interesting life than I could have concocted on my own. Years ago a person emerged from Duke Chapel, shaking, upset about my snide remark about Bill and Hillary, or maybe George and Laura. I can't remember. My critic got in a couple of jabs. As she buffeted me at the church door, a crowd gathered (students are invariably anticlerical). Yet, God help me, as I was being viciously, unjustly attacked, I thought, *I don't care.*

I marveled: I was elected president of my class every year since the seventh grade; no election was ever won by truth telling. In less than thirty years God has made me relatively truthful by calling me to be a preacher!

The great Wesleyan theological achievement was to link justification to sanctification, salvation by grace to growth in grace, promising not only rebirth but continuing reconstruction. A living God keeps remaking us even when we thought we were done. I'm not the most truthful, altruistic, nonracist person in the world, but, trust me, you wouldn't have wanted to know me before God got a grip.

As the movers packed us up to exit Alabama episcopacy, under orders from the conference attorney, I cowered in the recesses of the episcopal manse. Managing the multiple lawsuits in which I was named, the lawyer advised, "If you want to get back to North Carolina by Advent, don't answer the doorbell."

Meanwhile Patsy, being interviewed by the *Birmingham News*, was asked, "How did your husband surprise you?" She answered, "His courage, his dogged determination in the face of fierce, cowardly opposition, most of it from the clergy he was attempting to lead."

The coward in the basement, the boy who was scared to walk from Fork Shoals Road to my front porch, or venture into the woods once the gate opened, was being transformed, miracle of miracles, into a relatively courageous person. Proof: once we left Alabama Methodism, nobody ever invited us back.

I posted a framed copy of preacher King's "Letter from Birmingham Jail" in my episcopal office. Character formation occurred every time I looked at the letter that disruptive King addressed not to redneck Klansmen but to well-meaning but overly cautious, balance-loving white, liberal bishops like me who, despite their better angels, thought it more important for the church to be happy than faithful, and valued public order over public good. How easily people like me get it wrong; how disruptively God works to set us right.

6

Adventitious Preacher

The word of the LORD came unto me, saying, Before I formed thee in the belly, I knew thee; and before thou camest forth out of the womb I sanctified thee, and I ordained thee a prophet unto the nations. Then said I, Ah, Lord GOD! behold, I cannot speak: for I am a child. But the LORD said unto me, Say not, I am a child: for thou shalt go to all that I shall send thee, and whatsoever I command thee thou shalt speak. Be not afraid of their faces: for I am with thee to deliver thee, saith the LORD. Then the LORD put forth his hand, and touched my mouth. And the LORD said unto me, Behold, I have put my words in thy mouth. See, I have this day set thee over the nations and over the kingdoms, to root out, and to pull down, and to destroy, and to throw down, to build, and to plant. (Jeremiah 1:4–10)

"I have this day set thee over the nations and over the kingdoms, to root out, and to pull down, and to destroy, and to throw down, to build, and to plant." High expectations for the preaching future of a fetus, exaggerated confidence in public speech. Kingdoms built and destroyed by words?

Just the sort of linguistic pyrotechnics one expects from a God who creates something out of nothing with "And God said . . ." Whatever God wants, God does through nonviolent words. And guess who's God's field rep in these old-world-wrecking, new-world-evoking endeavors?

I'm a preacher, playing a public role to which none can aspire, a job impossible without external assistance, an accidental,

imposed comedic life not my own. A preacher is someone for whom public speaking is more difficult than for most people, not because of the audience but due to Jesus.

While I'm supposed to be more interested in what God thinks about my sermon than in merely human evaluation—here's sermon feedback I can't get out of my head:

"You took a text, read it resonantly, and then wisely kept your distance for the remainder of your sermon" (Peter Gomes). "Congratulations on not allowing Yale to stifle your reckless exegesis. Quite appealing" (Betty Achtemeier). "What do you mean by 'poor Ralph Waldo Emerson'? I admire Emerson" (President Nan Keohane). "Sir, you are an excellent communicator" (Ted Koppel). "How lucky to have you as our preacher" (President Keith Brodie). "Would that I had the opportunity to challenge your biblical interpretation" (N. T. Wright). "My son told me about you. Why the hell can't Catholics preach?" (Prime Minister Brian Mulroney). "Thanks for so eloquently reminding me why I could never be a Christian" (Duke undergrad). "Did you really say 'erection' when you meant 'resurrection'?" (Barbara Brown Taylor). "Polemic? No. I'd say it was more of a rant" (Richard Lischer). "'Grace' ran loose like a greased pig through that sermon" (Stanley Hauerwas). "What was that supposed to be?" (dean of African American preachers, Henry Mitchell). "Disregard Henry, I thought your sermon was wonderful" (Ella Mitchell). "How dare you? Our president is a good man!" (older man in a wheelchair). "If this doesn't work out for you, we could use a preacher like you in Plains" (Jimmy Carter). "My young adult son was here with us. Thanks for using 'orgasm' in a sermon" (Trustee Chair, Northside UMC). "Careful, old man! I work out at Crossfit" (Nadia Bolz-Weber). "Brother!" (Cornel West). "Bored, I looked at the chapel windows thinking, Jesus has come a hell of a long way from Bethlehem" (Will Campbell). "Janis Joplin quoted from the pulpit of Duke Chapel?" (David Buttrick). "Wit and wisdom, prophetic jabbing and pastoral nurturing, poetic soarings and country store musings" (Tom Long). "You're a liar, a liberal, and an apostate" (Bob Jones III).

Coach Mike Krzyzewski once advised, "You and me are alike."

How, pray tell?

"Both of us don't have to wait for feedback on how well we're doing."

Coach K and I are brothers in receiving immediate public acclaim or rebuke, though there are major discrepancies in our salaries.

*   *   *

On a Sunday in February 1984, two young adults showed up at Northside. Northside had few visitors; almost none were young.

I asked them the allegedly revelatory South Carolina lead question, "Where are you from?"

"Durham, North Carolina," they answered.

"Durham? I used to live there," I said. "What brings you guys to Greenville?"

"Just passing through," they responded. I should have been suspicious.

Over a decade later, in Duke Hospital ministering to the legendary Terry Sanford in his last days, I said, "Thanks, for giving me the best job a Methodist preacher could have. Thanks for taking a risk and hiring me at Duke Chapel."

From his bed Uncle Terry (as the students called him) said weakly, "Best thing I did for Duke was you. I'd never heard of you, of course. People warned me that all you wanted to do was to write books. I could tell you were more of a preacher than a professor first time you opened your mouth."

He gazed out the hospital window and sighed. "Seems like just yesterday those two students reported back to me about you. I had 'em call me during Sunday dinner as soon as your church got out in Greenville."

"You did what?" I asked.

"You think I'd hire a preacher at Duke Chapel without first finding out what students thought of you?"

It was then that I recalled the two anonymous young visitors back in '84.

"'The church he's at isn't much to look at,' they said. 'But he preached a right good sermon.'

"'So what was his text?' I asked 'em.

"'Jeremiah. First chapter. About how God made Jeremiah a prophet.'

"'What did the preacher say about it?' I asked.

"'He said everybody's supposed to be a prophet in one way or another. God wants everybody to speak up. Then he made a couple of wisecracks about President Bush,' they said.

"'Glad he's a Democrat,' I said. 'His sermon doesn't sound very original. Thought he might have taken that Jeremiah text in a different direction.'

"'We liked him. Thought he was real good,' they said."

Mr. Sanford grinned and looked from his bed toward me, noting my surprise. He continued: "'How many sermons have you boys heard?' I asked. 'Ya'll come on back to Durham and I'll get Preacher Willimon up here and check him out for myself.'"

Nobody is a preacher by parentage (no matter how good or how bad), life experience (horrible or wonderful), or natural gifts (few or many). No preacher was ever validated by matching the tangle of bean-counter ordination requirements in the UMC *Book of Discipline*. As Karl Barth said, only God can speak of God. Nobody but God authorizes truthful talk about God. If a preacher finds the words to bring the gospel to speech, it's only grace. "What do you have that you did not receive? . . . Why do you boast as if it were not a gift?" (1 Cor. 4:7, paraphrased). The Christian faith is inherently acoustical. You can't self-inoculate the gospel; somebody's got to tell it to you. It's auditory. As Paul said, faith comes through hearing (Rom. 10:17). And how will they hear without a preacher (Rom. 10:14)? This, the work God has assigned. Counting my time as bishop, I've preached more than two thousand sermons in over five hundred churches, massaging platitudes until they passed as profundities. There are eight hundred entries under my name at the Duke Sermon Archives website. If you count my two decades as writer for *Pulpit Resource*, add a thousand more. Calculate all the churches where subscribers repreached my *Pulpit Resource* sermons, and the number of people exposed to my proclamation increases geometrically. Had I known there would be so much public speaking, I would have responded to God's call in a more timely fashion. You'll have to ask these congregations what they thought of my preaching, but for me, as for Mae West, too much of a good thing has been wonderful.

My first week in Alabama I met with the president of the United Methodist Women. In our conversation I asked, "What is the most important thing I can do as your bishop?"

Mattie Battle, a retired educator, responded, "Preach well! And get rid of pastors who can't."

I told her that I was delighted to receive her commission. I love to preach and to teach about preaching.

Then Ms. Battle took my hand in hers and said, "You're new here. But let me tell you: it's too hard to be black in Alabama without being backed up by good preaching."

I vowed then and there, *I will not appoint a pastor to a congregation without having heard that pastor preach.* Every January I listened to over a hundred sermons on CD and then responded to each, attempting thereby to stress the importance of preaching. Listening to so many sermons was both inspiring (pastors in out-of-the-way places you will never hear of finding a way to bring the gospel to speech) and disheartening (pastors who vainly believed that empathetic, unctuous hand-holding made up for shoddy pulpit work).

By listening to sermons and visiting in a variety of preaching venues, I discovered that the church is the most supple, adaptable, inherently innovative human organization ever. Preaching in a little storefront church in Chicago, in a gigantic megachurch in Colorado, in a hut in San Marco, Honduras (*en español*), in a terrified downtown cathedral in Detroit, on a barren playground in Haiti, to a defiant twenty-something congregation renting a dead Lutheran church in Manhattan, to a disheartened parish in the Ruhr (*auf Deutsch*), and in a bar in Brooklyn that thinks it's a church on Sundays (I, their least hip preacher ever), I've experienced Jesus's absurdly malleable definition of church. Jesus has never found a people he couldn't speak to or a culture he was unable to disrupt to his advantage.

"Reverend, don't worry," my host shouted over a whooping Los Angeles congregation, "a spear carrier will have a cool-down robe for you right after you preach. Here's your towel."

I'm too old to be a Pentecostal.

In a Belfast Methodist church, as I studied photographs in the hallway before the processional, the pastor said, "Those folks were murdered either coming to or returning from church."

"The authorities keep kicking us out, so I won't know where you'll be preaching until just before I pick you up," said my host in Nanking. "Don't tell anybody at the hotel that you are a preacher."

Jesus is amazing.

Christ talks his way into even the most hostile situations, even one as adeptly atheist as Duke. Just give Jesus a preacher with the guts to work with a relentlessly encroaching savior, a congregation willing to be smacked with the gospel, and Jesus is off to the races.

"Friend, your prayer life has just improved," said an older bishop the night I was elected to the episcopacy. This was true. Each week I wrote a dozen of my six hundred pastors, telling them I would pray for each of them in the coming week, asking if there were challenges in their ministry that they would like me to lift up to God, forewarning that I had been praying against the Iraq war for years with no appreciable divine response. Each day I looked at the pastor's photo in the conference directory and prayed. Watching God work in the lives of many whom I would never have approved to be pastors expanded my appreciation for God's vocative resourcefulness.

*   *   *

Because I can never be sure that the ministerial positions to which I have aspired are not just Boy Scout merit badge acquisitions, the Lord has found ways to counter my aspirations with vocation. Rich and powerful Thomas Becket had always been a Christian, but when Becket was made archbishop the Lord worked in him a deep conversion. Wearing a monk's cowl and hair shirt under his princely robes, Becket thumbed his nose at the king and fiercely defended the prerogatives of the church. Being bishop changed me by exposure to dozens of Alabama crossroad churches where I got to preach the gospel and to see visible, tangible, bodily proof that Jesus Christ is Lord.

I was invited by a church outside Birmingham for their groundbreaking for a new fellowship hall. After stashing away funds for years, they were finally ready to begin construction. The preacher called the week before to say there had been a change of plans. A couple in the church who specialized in caring for special-needs children had expanded their family by four, receiving children for whom no homes could be found.

"So we prayed about it, and, bishop," the pastor explained, "we gave the whole building fund to buy 'em a bigger house. If you were planning to offer theological justification for that fellowship hall, you'll need to come up with a different sermon."

Years ago President Brodie asked me to study and then to report on student life at Duke after dark. I did rounds with the Duke police, moved into a dorm, interviewed student groups, crashed keg parties, and then wrote *We Work Hard; We Play Hard*. Later, President Keohane asked for a follow-up, *Old Duke, New Duke*. Those reports, along with my popularization of the terms "front loading" and "binge drinking," got me gigs at forty colleges and universities where I played the expert on all things alcohol. The president of the University of West Virginia introduced me, "This man knows more about student rowdiness than any preacher on the planet."

Amid my nightly research, I interacted with a Duke fraternity about alcohol and student life. "Why won't the administration leave us alone?" asked a frat boy. "Every week there's some new booze restriction. It's college! I should be free to experiment. If I get hammered on weekends, who cares?"

Under the influence of the Holy Spirit, I replied, "I read that beer consumption is declining in North America among every group of adults except one—students. That's why you never see anybody my age in a beer commercial. You think beer is validation of your freedom from your parents. I say that your overindulgence shows they still own you. How many drinks does it take your father to endure your mother at dinner?"

A guy called out, "Two."

"My question was rhetorical; obviously you have no experience with preachers. Alcohol induces you to believe that you are living the life you want when, in reality, some *Mad Men* dude pulls your strings."

"Man, you are cynical," they said.

The *Duke Chronicle*, in a screed after the publication of *We Work Hard; We Play Hard*, charged, "Willimon has made no real changes to the campus. It's just words."

"I'm a preacher!" I responded. "You're journalists! Words are we."

Duke's residential communities, faculty in dorms, library coffee shops and cafés, substance-free social options, and other expensive, positive changes in student life are the fruit of my reports. At least that's the way I see it, a preacher with nothing in my holster but words.

*   *   *

May I never cease being surprised that, of all people, I was enlisted to bring God's words to the world, Yeats's falconer listening for the cry of the falcon. Two years after my Marney-inspired "epiphany of recruitment" (Charles Taylor), I finally found the courage to admit to my mother that I was thinking about seminary. This news she received as if I had announced I was matriculating at Gandalf's School for Wizards.

"I'm sorry to hear that," she replied. "Preachers must cajole and flatter, soothe and patronize. Let's just say that's not your gift."

Years later, someone emerged from Duke Chapel after service whining, "I know you would never want to hurt anyone in a sermon, but I was deeply upset by your statement that . . ."

Mother warned me.

"It's a sermon, for God's sake! Hurt comes with the territory!" I hollered as my deprecator stormed away. "Luther said 'a sermon is a surgeon's scalpel!' Hey, he also said, 'Whenever the word of God is rightly preached, demons are unleashed!'" Luther, my go-to defender when I'm victimized by congregational faultfinding.

If you have witnessed my friend Jim Forbes or Gardner Taylor perform God's word, with copious alliteration, artistry, and numerous digressions, then you know why preaching is the superior language art. I wish you could have heard my guest Jerry Falwell seduce a hostile student audience at Duke by name-dropping—in which Jerry bragged of his intimacies with every liberal icon. ("So like I said to Coretta . . ." and "I told Teddy Kennedy . . .") In five minutes Jerry had them eating out of his hand.

"Atheism oughta be of sterner stuff," I rebuked the students as they applauded Jerry.

You can't read a sermon; you must be bodily present for the aural event, live. Fragile. Occasional. Particular. In a sense, all sermons are *ex tempore*. The Holy Spirit loves nothing better (thank God) than to rip a sermon out of a preacher's hands and romp wildly in the congregation so that maybe someone says to you at the door, "After that sermon, if I die right now, it's OK," or even, "I was so deeply upset that I . . ."

I lacked the courage to try drugs in college, but surely uppers give no greater high than Sunday morning as I rise and declaim to a defenseless congregation, "Get ready to hear a word you've avoided all week." Quite a rush. Like heroin (so I hear).

Reprimanded by the president for a wisecrack about Microsoft (presidents hate angry letters from alumni), "Why do you say the things you say in sermons?," I defended myself: "I fear boredom more than heresy. They said nasty things about Jesus. Nobody ever said he was dull."

"That makes no sense," she responded. A really good comeback came to mind, something about my being a better friend of Jesus than she, but remembering whose name was on my paycheck, I benignly smiled.

It is great freedom for a preacher to have a keen sense of vocation. God, not my listeners, owns my words. While I crave congregational approval, that's not what ultimately counts. Say unto them (if you have no need of a monthly paycheck), "Got a problem with my sermon? Take it up with the Lord."

*   *   *

Looking back upon your life, said Augustine, it's as if you are gazing into a chicken pen with hundreds of random chicken tracks in the mud. But then, if you look through the eyes of faith, you begin to discern pattern, direction, and beauty that were there all along.

I'm that rare codger who looks back upon life's twists and turns and says, *Thanks.* By God's grace, it was for the good.

When students reported some disappointment, I comforted them with talk of inscrutable but ultimately beneficent Providence, telling them how, when I applied to graduate school at Duke, armed with recommendations from three Yale professors, I was rejected. Crushed, I applied to Emory, where I had a wonderful graduate experience anyway.

"Sometimes God works justice in payment for the slings and arrows of incompetent admissions committees," I reassured students. Demanding and generous Duke hired me not once but thrice.

"If that admissions committee had not rejected me in the spring of '71," I told Dean Langford in '76, "you could have gotten me for ten thousand less."

*   *   *

"God can ride a lame horse or shoot with a crooked bow," said Luther. By God's grace, even life's setbacks can be used by God to re-call a preacher. Wofford handed me not only an adequate education but also a humiliating rejection. I had been a finalist for the presidency of three colleges, so when Wofford needed a president, it seemed only right to me, and to my friends, that I should be the next. I had a list of good reasons for my candidacy and made a detailed presentation of how I would add value to the college as its first alumnus president. I should have expected a letdown. The search committee dozed through my interview, asked three impertinent questions, and then billed me for my motel room. When I got the call from the committee removing me from the process (the first time in a presidency search that I failed to make the top three), I was crushed. Immediately I assembled reasons for this blow: South Carolina provincialism, the envy of fellow clergy, a key committee member's alcoholism, faculty banality and insecurity, Spartanburg right-wingers' control of the college, and less charitable explanations.

In humiliation I called Duke's president. "Sorry, I didn't get the job at Wofford. You'll have to put up with me a bit longer."

"What did you say to upset them?" she asked, helpfully.

The day I was dumped from the Wofford search, I sat catatonically behind my Gothic desk in the Dean's Study in Duke Chapel, cursing myself for my involvement in the train wreck of a search. My only consolation was my uncle's "My boy, experience, you will find, is a most vauable teacha. If hit don't kill you."

A rap at the door. A student—from Ohio—bolted in, saying, "We need to talk."

"Not now," I said. "Bad time." Me, dead dog at the bottom of the well, once again boy without a tie or a daddy.

"Bad time for you?" he scoffed. "Wait 'til you hear what's happened to me. Come on, we can walk in Duke Gardens as we talk. Daffodils in bloom. You'll want to hear this."

He literally led me out of the chapel and into the gardens where he talked nonstop about changing his major, coming out of the closet, his misgivings about US foreign policy in Iraq, the salubrious properties of kale, and whether or not he should be baptized as Greek Orthodox.

Occasionally I inserted a "No" or "Why not?" or "That's stupid." (Pastoral care wasn't my best subject in seminary.)

As we walked back to my office, I confessed my dismay at being dumped by Wofford. Charlie responded, "Will, what the hell were you thinking? You mean to tell me you would walk off the best job in the world—talking to people like me about a God like the Holy Trinity, acting up in Jesus's name—throw away all that to be a damn small college president? Were you drunk?"

Wofford's past word was heard afresh: a Methodist preacher is all you will ever be.

*   *   *

Courting Patsy, I attended church with her family one Sunday. I was nervous because, unlike the Parkers, my family took church in small doses. Mr. Parker was then serving as the Marion District Superintendent. We paraded like ducks behind Mr. Parker to beige-bricked First Methodist Church. I had been warned that Carl Parker was miserable being consigned to a pew, forced to listen to another preach. The church's sad little pastor appeared to be jittery about preaching to the D.S. and his family plus the boyfriend.

"We need to be more committed to Christ!" he said, hastily adding, "I don't mean to the point of fanaticism, or to the neglect of family responsibilities. We are not Baptists, after all." He guffawed apprehensively. None in the congregation returned his laugh.

"We must be more involved in the church, though many of you lead busy lives and sometimes it's just impossible to be present. . . . I pray for a rebirth of good old Methodist piety, but not the showy sort. Nobody likes religion worn on the sleeve."

Bunyan's "Mr. Facing-Both-Ways" ricocheted on, one retrieval after another, with Carl Parker exaggeratedly, repeatedly pulling out his railroad pocket watch, looking at the time, shaking his head, and thrusting it back in his vest pocket with an audible sigh.

After the sermon finally rolled over and died, we paraded out, Mr. Parker barely acknowledging the preacher. We walked single file back to the district parsonage. Preacher Parker slung open the front door and stomped up the stairs toward his bedroom, ripping off his tie. On his way up he wheeled on the landing, seething, shaking his finger at me. "Boy, let me tell you one thing. If God should call you into the ministry, and if you go to seminary . . ."

"Yes sir?"

"And if you are ordained, and if the bishop entrusts you with a congregation, and if God gives you something to say, *for God sakes would you say it!*"

*   *   *

I'm old enough to remember when preachers were expected to be good with Scripture. These days we're cast into the role of experts doling out advice on marriage, business, the purpose-driven life, legislated justice, and sexual satisfaction. A lot of the preaching I hear today (and not only in a former stadium in Houston) is good advice; sentimental, worldly wisdom substituted for gospel foolishness; helpful hints for homemakers; tips for the anxious upwardly mobile; common sense widely available without having to get dressed and come to church to hear it. At least Rotary serves lunch.

In the temptations of Jesus, it was the devil who proffered common sense. Sanctimonious advice, even well meaning, is a bore. Most commonsense sermons—platitudes and principles foisted upon the congregation as if the preacher were an expert on life—are offered in the attempt to help us retain control over our lives by using common sense to keep a living God at bay. Preachers ought to remember the audience's elation when Hamlet's uncle—tedious, bloated-with-advice Polonius—finally gets a knife to the gut.

Thus I interrupted no more than a dozen sermons to condemn Trump's kleptocracy. Low hanging fruit. Besides, when Hitler rose to power in Germany, Karl Barth urged preachers to "preach as if nothing happened" and not to squander pulpit time on a political nothing when they could be offering Christ. Gospel preachers raise their artillery above the trenches of immediate relevance, said Barth, aiming at something of eternal significance.

The toughest sermons I've preached were occasioned by some tragic death. As a young pastor, I sat in my study an hour before the funeral for a child in the congregation, threatening the Lord: *I'm not going out there and make some poetic excuse for your behavior.*

By the time the prelude began, Jesus advised Romans 8 and letting Paul do the talking. Though at that moment I myself was not sure, it was good to hear Paul say that he was "convinced that nothing shall separate us from the love of Jesus Christ." Sometimes the one most in need of convincing is the preacher.

* * *

Preachers take criticism more seriously than praise, knowing that Jesus may have put denigrators up to it. Just when I think I've finally mastered the arts of ministry, the Lord forces me to hear sermon response that sends me back to the little league. While I was awaiting the procession into a Chicago ballroom at the convention of the Evangelical Covenant Church, a woman rushed up and said, "I've driven all the way from Dubuque to hear you. I love everything you write."

All the way from Dubuque? As the orchestra pounced on the processional hymn, even my inflated ego managed to swell. *All the way from Dubuque?* resounded in my soul.

I preached, they sang, we recessed into the lobby. The same person came up, deflated, and said, "You aren't Frederick Buechner!"

Some years ago an inmate in the state penitentiary wrote to tell me that by radio he had listened to my sermons from Duke Chapel. We began correspondence. He lauded my direct, "in-your-face" pulpit style; for the first time he was beginning to love Scripture because my sermons had helped him "recover a sense that I'm a cherished child of God."

No sweeter sound to a preacher's ears. True, he had time on his hands to sit through my sermons, but still, that's treasured praise. My grateful listener was serving a life sentence for splitting the skull of his mother with an ax. For any of his faults, he knew a good sermon when he heard it.

* * *

Though I relished preaching at prestigious pulpits like Riverside in New York, Memorial Church at Harvard, and the National Cathedral, nowhere I've preached was more intimidating than the little church in Alabama where, Easter week, a tornado tore through and ripped the walls off their beloved sanctuary.

Amid the ruin I got to give testimony to a fearful huddle of people who asked, "Is there any word from the Lord?"

It occurred to me that it has been my lot, as a leader of a mainline Protestant church, to preach amid the ruins of a desolated church nearly every Sunday.

On a cold March day, I threw my voice into the void of Rockefeller Chapel, University of Chicago. No response from the frozen few. "I'm okay if you don't invite me back," I told the depressed dean afterward. "My faith is too fragile."

I proudly showed Bishop Emilio de Carvalho around Duke Chapel one morning. He was impressed by the million pieces of stained glass in the windows. Bishop de Carvalho gave heroic witness during Angola's revolution. "We told our pastors when they were arrested, 'Don't crowd in one cell. Spread out! So you can better evangelize.' As you know, hymns are the best way to attract converts in jail. Only a dozen of our pastors were executed."

"Have a pleasant trip from Angola to Durham?" I asked evasively.

"I was baptizing on a river in Angola. The pastor said we would have twenty. We had a hundred! I baptized as fast as I could, but it grew late. I said I must leave for America. The people began shouting, throwing things. The pastor got a loudspeaker and calmed them. I said, 'Two weeks. I come back. Baptize the rest.'"

"Wow."

"How many you baptize each year at Duke?" he asked.

"Well, er, uh, it's a university chapel, so not many. But I think we had maybe four baptisms last year," I answered.

"Forty? Four hundred?" asked the bishop.

"Four."

"Inspiring."

Inspiring? Maybe he's having trouble with his third language.

Bishop Carvalho embraced me as he said, "I tell you this. When I return to Angola, I will tell the sisters and brothers that in America I met a man who stands up every Sunday and preaches the gospel, even though God has given him no fruit."

*   *   *

Any preacher who hands over the gospel within the limited confines of a relatively affluent, content congregation has good gospel reason to be *en garde*. Still, the gospel of Jesus Christ thrives even when cast upon rocky soil (Matt. 13). God's words will "not return empty" (Isa. 55:11), which we preachers don't know whether to take as a promise or a threat.

Joining my preachers for a morning of ministry in the maximum security prison outside Birmingham, I timidly approached a man on death row. From previous prison work I knew not to ask what he was in for or how his family was doing. He broke the ice. "So you're a Methodist preacher? I once was a Methodist, now I'm a Baptist."

Don't brag; there are millions like you.

"Methodists stress incarnation more than they preach atonement or justification. How often do you preach the blood of Jesus?"

"How's the food here?" I hastily asked.

Sad to say, my preaching shows atonement deficit. Is that because I'm preaching to people who don't know they're on death row? For the not-too-afflicted, not-overly-anxious, good old Methodist, moralistic, sentimentally therapeutic Deism is gospel enough. Not long ago a sermon was inflicted upon us in which the preacher urged us to "wrap the shawl of love around yourself," to move from the "house of fear to the house of love." When Methodism loses a redemptive, active God, this is what you get: suffocatingly sappy hokum. Sentimentality is Methodism's go-to gospel substitute. God is okay with you just as you are; no need to submit to baptismal *metanoia*, conversion, and detoxification.

Thank God I got to be bishop in Alabama. It's theologically invigorating to be around Methodists who can't deny their complicity with evil. Life in a state where one-third of African American men between eighteen and thirty are incarcerated or permanently disenfranchised strengthens one's hamartiology. Woe to the church that thinks it can substitute Bible talk of judgment, reparations, and mercy with blather about shawls and "love."

*   *   *

On a summer Sunday in 1991 I preached in the Ruhr in a severe postwar German church building. An older woman showed me through the church's history room.

"That was our church," she said, proudly pointing to a photograph of a neo-Gothic church with a tall steeple. "It was destroyed by American bombing in 1944."

I preached uneasily that Sunday on Luke 15.

On the Tuesday after that I was digging in the archives of the *Kirchenkampf*, the struggle of the German churches with National Socialism. I came across a folder from that very congregation that contained mimeographed copies of church newsletters from the forties. The first one I pulled out included a weekly message from the pastor to the congregation entitled "Does Salvation Come from the Jews?" The pastor had given a biblical, learned *Nein!* He explained, using the best resources of nineteenth-century Continental biblical criticism, how the Jews had killed Christ and had thus excluded themselves from salvation. A chill went down my spine.

Some congregations get the preaching they deserve. We preachers form a congregation through our sermons, but congregations also form us. One morning I opened a small, powder blue envelope addressed with a flowery hand that I knew to be that of one of our older women at Duke Chapel. Folded within the note was a newspaper clipping that reported that American troops had buried alive a score of Iraqi soldiers in their trenches during a battle.

"By the time we got there, nothing but arms and hands sticking out of the sand," said one GI.

"Did you preach on this?" she asked in her note. "I don't get out much anymore but I listen to your sermons on television and I don't recall that you mentioned this atrocity. Where is the moral voice of our clergy? We are frighteningly dependent upon our preachers."

With your help, Alice Philips, one day I might become a faithful preacher.

*   *   *

A Duke frat asked me to their housing section to talk on any subject for twenty minutes on a Thursday night.

"Why me?" I asked.

"Some of the guys say you are hip and don't talk too long. There was a misunderstanding at a party. The damn dean put us on probation and required us to have fifteen hours of cultural programming before we can have another party. Doesn't matter what the program is about. So we thought of you."

Thou hast delivered mine enemies into my hands (Josh. 10:8).

At 8:00 p.m. I pressed the buzzer outside the fraternity section. I was stunned by a young child who opened the door.

"You the preacher?" he asked.

A little boy at a Duke fraternity on a Thursday night?

"They're waiting for you." The child led me down a dark labyrinth to the commons room. There I was greeted by a silent huddle of men with their hands in their sweatpants, staring disinterestedly at the ceiling.

I launched into an exposition of the notion of friendship. I watched as the child climbed into the lap of the president and went to sleep. Twenty minutes later I asked, "Any reactions to my presentation?"

Zombie-like stares. So I said, "This has been wonderful, but now I'll head back to suburbia. Best wishes in your life journeys. No need to invite me ever again."

I watched as the president awakened the little boy and said, "Tyrone, go brush your teeth and put on your pajamas, and I'll come read you a story."

The heavily inked president escorted me out. Once outside, he lit a cigarette, took a long drag. "I liked some of the things you said."

"Look, who was that child there tonight?" I demanded.

"Oh, that's Tyrone."

"What in God's name was he doing there at this time of night in a student dorm?"

"We got to know Tyrone and his mother through our chapter's Big Brother Program. She's got that crack monkey on her back. She's trying. Sometimes she's okay, and when she's not, we get Tyrone. We bought him a phone so he can call us anytime. He stays for a night or two, sometimes as long as a couple of weeks. We buy his books, clothes, and get him to school."

"Er, uh, I retract what I said about your being immoral and immature. That's just wonderful," I said, sheepishly.

He took another drag, blew a cloud of smoke, and said, "I'll tell you what's wonderful: God Almighty chose somebody like me to do something this good for somebody else. That's wonderful."

That evening, who preached to whom?

*   *   *

In a 1972 concert in Israel, Leonard Cohen became frustrated with his performance. He walked off the stage and dropped some acid to gain confidence. From backstage he heard the audience singing "*Shalom Aleichem.*" The audience had sensed Cohen's disappointment with himself, so they were singing him back on stage. Cohen said later, "The entire audience turned into one Jew," singing to the one who was attempting to sing to them.

Congregations have preached me back into the pulpit after a DOA sermon. Sometimes the church sings the gospel you find difficult until you're ready again to pick up the tune.

"Where do you get these stories?" a student asked after my cute sermon on Matthew 20, the laborers in the vineyard.

"Stories? I guess from growing up in South Carolina," I replied.

"I was troubled by the one today. That's no way to treat people, paying everyone the same wage regardless of how little they worked. It's an injustice."

"Hey," I said, "that story's not original with me. That's Matthew."

"Matthew?"

"It's in the Bible," I explained.

"Oh, the Bible. Yes."

"What's your religious background?" I asked, praying to God she wouldn't say Methodist.

"Maybe we went to a Presbyterian church, I think, when I was young."

"I envy you," I told her. "I work with this stuff so much it goes limp. I've preached an outrageous story from Jesus and a thousand people have told me that my sermon made sense. You, on the other hand, are outraged, offended. Quite an intellectual achievement in the context of moderate, mainline religion. Just for your information, that guy was murdered a few weeks later for telling that story."

*   *   *

After my sermon on the preexistence of Christ, in which I bounced John 1 off Philippians 2, a student responded, "I didn't know we believed that stuff. Awesome! That's like Mormons or the Moonies."

Next in line, Stanley Hauerwas. "Congratulations. Your sermon was completely irrelevant. That's a homiletical success among this crowd of instrumentalists and utilitarians."

I went home to Sunday dinner happy, wishing the uncles would be there to debate the sermon's merits.

Still, there are too many Sundays when I'm up there flailing away, going down for the third time, pouring out my heart and receiving nothing from the congregation, the Holy Spirit having taken the Sunday off. They are Helen Keller and I'm Annie Sullivan, feverishly pumping, making letters in their palms with my fingers, and shouting WATER! WATER!

When composing a sermon, I apply a theological test: *What is God doing in this biblical text, and what might God condescend to do in my sermon?* Preaching arises from the conviction that Christ really is present, or could likely show up, in Word and sacrament, speaking for himself, walking freely among his people (Bonhoeffer's definition of preaching). Christ, the only preacher. In spite of generations of homiletics professors, no one has been able to devise a preaching method so lousy that it keeps the Trinity from insinuating herself into preaching. Every biblical text, even the most prosaic, God can use as an excuse to take on our assorted idolatries. In my sorriest sermons, Jesus may elect to preach.

Each fall Proverbs makes a brief appearance in the lectionary. I don't care for Proverbs—insufferably Ben Franklinesque moralistic exhortations of early to bed, early to rise, don't drink too much, take precautions on dates, pick up your socks (reminding one of a long road trip with mother). No God in Proverbs; if you are good enough to obey all those maxims, you need neither forgiveness nor salvation; go worship maxims rather than Jesus. Nevertheless, I did a non-Methodist thing: I stuck with the text, Proverbs 22:1, "A good name is rather to be chosen than great riches."

I noted that, unlike the university, Proverbs doesn't shrink from value judgments: "Hey, kid, this way leads to a life worth living; that way to death."

"Nice thought. Except nobody has matriculated here to get a good name. We go for the gold. Somebody get the Donald on the phone and ask, 'Hey, I'm a college student and wondering, what's the life worth living? I could try for a good name or I could act like you. What do you advise?'" (Note: My sermon was preached back in Trump's adulterer/casino days, long before his birther movement. Not to brag, but I was the first to condemn the rascal from a pulpit, September 1993, prior to others piling on.)

"Put Proverbs 22:1 on a T-shirt. Wear it on campus this week. Let me know how you do in fraternity rush." And so on.

At the end of the service, a young man emerged, thanking me for my "pastoral sermon." *Pastoral? I aimed for obnoxious.*

"Such a comfort. I'm calling my dad tonight to tell him that I'm not applying to law school. I'm going into elementary teaching, and if he doesn't like it he can go to hell."

"Don't mention my name when you call," I yelled to him as he left. "And don't tell him where you were at 11:30 this morning!"

Isn't that wonderful? God took a trivial, anthropological, hortatory text and made it theological. God used a cowardly, compromised, Southern-accented preacher to speak for God, so determined is Jesus to have his say. Paul was not indulging in hyperbole when he wrote, "Not I, but Christ liveth in me" (Gal. 2:20).

*   *   *

My first attempt at a sermon was while I was a summer youth pastor at Trinity UMC in Anderson, South Carolina, '68. Of course, I attacked Lyndon Johnson (maybe Lady Bird too), and of course, I assailed the then-current Vietnam War.

After service, an enraged man shouted at the church door, "Punks like you are the shame of America" and "You are a cowardly little pussy who doesn't support our boys fighting in Southeast Asia."

"I'll have you know I was a Distinguished Military Student at Wofford," I protested. "You're looking at a second lieutenant, armor, though I never saw a tank." My lame defense served only to inflame. I was unsure whether to protect my face, my stomach, or my groin.

I staggered back into the church, getting as far as the vestry. A member of the altar guild, an older woman in a small pink hat, was removing flowers from the brass vases.

"That was awful!" I gasped. "Did you hear what he said to me?"

"I think everyone heard," she said. "I do wish people wouldn't use such language when children are present. Could you hand me that container?"

"You and me both. He was going to hit me! How could that jerk be that upset by a first-year seminarian trying to preach?"

She looked up from fussing with flowers and said, "Dear, it's not you who upset him. I'm sure you remind him of his son. Both of you have long hair, though you appear to have no tattoos or ear piercing. Tommy is a homosexual, living in California or somewhere like that. He's lost the son to whom he gave his life. Tom kept his promise to God to be a good father, but God failed to keep his promise to Tom."

She laughed to herself. "Now, who would be upset with a nice boy like you? No, Tom hates *God*."

As I staggered out of the vestry, she said sweetly, "Everyone is so grateful that such a nice young man is willing to put himself at God's disposal. Good luck."

Some congregations get the preaching they deserve.

*   *   *

One of the best things about being a preacher is that one preaches from, rather than apologizes for, a biblical text. Praised be the Bible—big (too long), richly varied (poorly edited), audacious (every sacred cow and pompous person fair game), uncooperative (not a single instance of self-defense or economic success in the whole New Testament), and odd. Most preachers have a love/hate relationship with the sheer strangeness, the distance that Scripture asserts even as it brings God near. As literary critic Erich Auerbach said, "Scripture is more difficult than it ought to be."

While the Bible is a human product, there's no way that we could have come up with Scripture on our own. God wheedles into and unveils from Scripture as nowhere else. Though I've preached thousands of sermons on as many biblical passages, the lid will be screwed down on me in the chapel crypt before I do justice to the Bible's luxuriousness. Even though I read Scripture every day, vast portions are still *terra incognita*. Only a fool would wander alone in Daniel or Lamentations without the reassuring protection of a first-class biblical commentary to explain urbanely that, while God may have said some strange things to some Jews back then, there's no way that God would say stuff like that to thoughtful, educated people today.

For preachers, Scripture is a continually renewable resource. Scott Fitzgerald's "The Crack-Up" records the loss of his vocation as a writer. Fitzgerald attributes his fall to his foolishly "drawing on resources that I did not possess," "mortgaging myself physically and spiritually up to the hilt." Of the twenty people who were ordained with me, only two of us made it to retirement as clergy. A major reason for burnout or blackout among clergy, from what I've seen as bishop, is failure to allow the text to fund and fuel our preaching and thereby rescue us from the grinding mundanity of parish ministry.

I've been at biblical interpretation for five decades, and I'm grateful that Jesus still uses a text to jolt and jostle. Left to our own devices, we wouldn't have dared devise the Trinity. Down through the ages we have shown ourselves capable of thinking up godlets easier to get along with than Jesus.

*　　　　*　　　　*

The best sermonic moments occur as manna dropped from heaven accidentally, serendipitously. I've mentioned my fondness for Birmingham's Church of the Reconciler—church for, by, and with the homeless. The first time I preached at Church of the Rec, after the Call to Worship, I gazed at the gathering gleaned off the city streets and realized that my proposed sermon was a stupid mistake. I tossed my sermon and prayed, "Come on, Lord, give me something. I'm dying down here. You owe me. Line!" That frantic prayer, though prayed often, has rarely been answered—the Lord builds character by having a preacher publicly experience being "poor in spirit." But that day, with a congregation of the wretched of the streets before me, the Holy Spirit fed me the words.

"It's always a blessing to be with you," I began. "Now the question for this morning is: What did Jesus do for a living? What line of work was he in?"

Silence. Finally someone ventured, "Carpentry?"

"Good guess. No. His daddy Joseph was a carpenter, but no record of Jesus ever helping out in the shop."

"A preacher?" tried another.

"Right! But back then, people didn't yet know that you could defang a preacher with a good salary and a fat pension. No, Jesus couldn't have earned a living wage by preaching."

"Did Jesus have an apartment?" somebody called out.

"Great question!" I said. "Nothing about Jesus working, but we do know that 'even foxes have holes to crawl into at night but the Son of Man has nowhere to lay his head.'

"Here's the truth: Jesus Christ was an unemployed, homeless beggar . . . that's why he accepted so many dinner invitations, even to homes where he wasn't liked. He was hungry and had nowhere else to go."

Somebody down front shouted, "That's all right, Jesus! I ain't got no job neither! That's all right!" Applause in the congregation. "That's all right!"

"No job, no house, no nothin', just like Jesus!" shouted a woman who danced in the aisle as the band struck up. General applause and adoration from the assembly.

A few raucous minutes later, I waved the congregation to silence. "You've got my drift. Christians believe that a homeless (drumroll), jobless ('Amen!') Jew ('Go ahead!') is the whole truth about who God is and what God is up to.

"So," I shouted above the joyful din, "that means that even with degrees from Yale and Emory, even though I can read this stuff in Greek, some of you are closer to Jesus than your bishop!" Dancing and shouting resumed.

My best sermon, a Holy Spirit–induced accident.

Preaching is judged by its performance in the lives of the saints. I left teaching at Duke Divinity School the first time because the preacher in me knew that the test of the Christian faith is not the thoughts it generates but its corporate embodiment.

"Let me clarify for you students who are new at the university," I said one Opening Sunday. "Duke Chapel is not the Department of Religious Studies. They sit back and think religion; we enjoy *doing it*. Thank God they aren't the Department of Sex, or none of us would be here!"

Another letter from the president. Another groveling apology from me.

Visiting an ailing octogenarian in my congregation as she lay in hospital, I asked what she would like me to pray for.

"Pray that my young doctor will leave me alone. That silly boy intends to subject me to therapy that he alleges would give me another two years! If I were twenty, I would take up the offer. Why consume resources of those who are younger? It's not 'health care'; it's death denial. No thanks, I've had quite enough."

I left her hospital room thinking, Baylor was right. I truly am one of the most effective preachers in the English-speaking world.

*   *   *

One summer morning, while teaching in Münster in 1991, I scurried to the Kaufhof, taking my electric razor so that I might purchase new blades. Rushing from floor to floor—in just a few hours I was to give a lecture—I grabbed this and that.

As I was making my way to the electronics counter, two thuggish, unshaven men, dressed in black leather, stepped in front of me.

"Hast du etwas vergessen?" one asked. (Have you forgotten something?)

No.

"Sind Sie hollander?" (Are you Dutch?)

I responded in confusion. "Nein, ich bin Amerikaner. Gastprofessor hier. Why do you ask?"

"Haben Sie vergessen, etwas zu bezahlen?" (Have you forgotten to pay for something?)

"Nein!" I showed them the goods in my bag. "I haven't paid because I'm not yet leaving the store."

"Du hast die Abteilung verlassen!" (You have left the *Abteilung*!)

Abteilung? Abteilung? Panicked, I rummaged through the German-English dictionary in my head. What the heck is *Abteilung*?

It turns out that German law says one must pay for goods in the section in which the goods are displayed before moving to another department. My pleas went unheeded. In a few minutes two grim *Polizei* led me to the Münster police station where I was booked: *Ladendiebstahl*, shoplifting.

Film noir scenes of uniformed Germans came to mind as I trudged back to the Uni. My host professor attempted to reason with the department store. They had me on film leaving the section without paying. A lawyer was obtained. For the first time in my life, I was utterly dependent upon another to get me out of a legal jam.

I met with the lawyer, and he declared that he could spring me on the basis of *Sprache Missverständnis*, language ineptitude. Pride at my mastery of German wilted.

At our last meeting, the attorney gave me a book of paintings of the few Münster sites that survived British and American bombing. "Herr Professor Villemon, I apologize for 'dis affair. History is a teacher with no students. Please dink vell of us ven you remember Münster."

Though harrowing, I got a bang-up sermon out of it, a meditation on 1 John 2:1, "If [anyone sins], we have an advocate (*paraklētos*) with the Father, Jesus Christ." I preached that the text paid the Trinity high compliment in calling the Holy Spirit a lawyer. Thank God we don't have to argue our case before the Almighty. Jesus will find just the right words to advocate eloquently in our behalf.

That's another joy of being a preacher: even the worst moments become grist for the mill that accidentally produces a sermon.

Nothing bad ever happens to a preacher.

7

Serendipitous Writer

Forasmuch as many have taken in hand to set forth . . .
those things which are most surely believed among us, . . . it
seemed good to me also . . . to write unto thee in order, most
excellent Theophilus, that thou mightest know the certainty
of those things, wherein thou hast been instructed. (Luke
1:1–4)

So far as I know, Jesus neither read nor wrote a book. Yet from the first, many wrote about him. Sometime in the first century, somewhere in the Levant, somebody named Mark invented something called a gospel. A bit biography, a bit history, sort of, a gospel is best read as a sermon. Mark has no interest in the modern, "Is there a God?" Mark's question is vocational, "What is Jesus, Son of God, up to, and how can I entice you to hitch on?" Using an impressive array of literary devices, tropes, and conceits, Mark writes for propagation, conversion, enlistment, vocation to a way nobody wants to walk.

Like Luke writing to Theophilus, a.k.a. Lover of God (Luke 1:3), it's my good fortune to be a preacher who publishes: preacher by vocation, writer by inclination and avocation. I got the call to write before I was called to preach. The week before our grand trek from Greenville to Colorado Springs for the 1960 National Jamboree, Scouts of the Blue Ridge Council received last-minute instruction. Scout executives announced the lackeys whom they had tapped for senior patrol leader, chaplain, patrol leaders, and quartermaster. "Williamson? Williston? Willerman? You are troop scribe." *Scribe? What's that?* "You write reports to the chief scout executive. He'll send them to the *Greenville News* if they're newsworthy." *What's "newsworthy"?* As our overburdened, dilapidated buses belched through Kentucky, I got the guts to ask the scoutmaster why I had been selected as scribe. "The popular boys were chosen as troop leaders," he explained. "You gotta take what's left."

Every couple of days I dutifully mailed my dispatches to Mr. Stanley. Knowing that old man Stanley hired the ancient buses that broke down in Oklahoma, I described eighty boys sweltering on the side of the road awaiting a mechanic. Thank God for the first aid merit badge, I wrote, or we could have died in Soonerland. I quoted comments about Stanley's logistical mismanagement. I informed my readers of the wasteland between Louisville and Colorado Springs; don't bother taking the trip. I testified to the rundown motel in Missouri where we were delighted by the pool but unhappy about being awakened throughout the night by men banging on our doors calling out, "Myrtle? Are you in there? I paid! Myrtle? It's my time." I disclosed how Henry Taylor—who had climbed on the roof to retrieve his hatchet that had been thrown out the window during an argument—was locked out and forced to shiver in his briefs on the roof of Bates Motel until dawn.

Once at the Jamboree, I described the stew made by Scouts from the Congo—a week's rations dumped in one smoldering pot from which they ladled three brownish meals a day, reasoning, "It all goes to the same stomach." I marveled that Scouts from Texas conned New Yorkers out of fully embroidered Order of the Arrow patches, swapping them for horned toads that they swore made you hallucinate if you licked them.

I exposed the Scouts from Georgia who traded cockleburs nestled in small boxes of cotton to unsuspecting dolts from New Jersey as "Genuine Porcupine Eggs. Keep at 71 degrees for two weeks." I noted that President Eisenhower looked too old to be running the country, and that the Scouts from Laurens were vowing never to get back on the Buses of Death even if they had to break up with their girlfriends and stay in Colorado through high school.

When we finally limped back home (including the Scouts from Laurens, who were forced on the bus by a scoutmaster screaming, "I don't give a rip who your old man is!"), a crowd welcomed us at the Trailways Bus Depot. A reporter among them shouted, "Which one of you is, pardon my alliteration, *William Willimon*?" He waved a wad of clippings from the *Greenville News* with headlines "Scouts' Travail in Tennessee" and "Scouts Unimpressed by Presidential Visit."

"Hey, Walter Winchell Willimon. Your column got moved from the last page to the front after your second posting! How 'bout a big smile for your readers? The newsroom heard them northerners are still sittin' on them porcupine eggs. What'd you Scouts think of that whorehouse in Missouri?"

My mother said little on the way home except "Next time you

engage in journalism, remember that, unlike you, I'm staying in Greenville." *I'll write my way out.*

"Servants of the Word" was Luther's favorite designation for clergy, those enthralled to the Word Made Flesh—Jesus. Preachers work in words because God condescends to human speech. God has not given Christians an army to have our way in the world. *I wish.* All we've got is nonviolent, often inadequate, fragile, yet world-changing, life-giving words. The medieval author of *Cloud of Unknowing* said, "I don't mind at all if the loud-mouthed, . . . flatterers, . . . or fault-finders, gossips, . . . or talebearers . . . never see this book. I never meant to write for them. So they can keep out of it." As a gospel preacher of public truth, I'm not permitted so exclusive a readership. In her essay on vocation, "Why Work?," Dorothy Sayers says that "vocation" properly applies to fanatics whose lives are subservient to their work—writers and priests. To be consigned to both crazed callings has been my happy lot.

✳ ✳ ✳

I know what Thomas Mann is talking about when he says a writer is "someone for whom being a writer is more difficult than for most people." Yet I have found that authorship difficulties can be over-

come if you are writing for God. By God's grace, reading even a book as modest as this can be revelation in the hands of a God who calls. The Holy Spirit makes books talk. How typical of a God determined to be in relationship to breathe us a book, the Bible, constantly to be in vocational conversation.

We read not to be alone, says Proust. You are reading and the author exposes a long-buried thought so deep that you didn't consciously know you had thought it. It's then that a hand reaches from the page and takes your hand, and you know that you are not by yourself.

Because Jesus is often the cause, rather than the cure, of loneliness (Jer. 15:7), my writings are less about handholding than evangelism—mobilization, conscription, saying something that God might deign useful in someone's disruption.

∗   ∗   ∗

Augustine dismissed his early life as a rhetorician as training to be a "peddler of words." I'm okay with that on my tombstone. The future belongs to the word merchant who says, in a cogent, compelling way, what's really going on. Build your monuments, live your prominent life, accumulate stuff, gain power over others, get elected to office . . . and then this Methodist preacher will write about you, tell some truth, go public in print, stand up at your funeral and offer the benediction, have the last word.

Writing—in print, walking naked down Main Street—is a perilous avocation. My sophomore year I was elevated to art editor for the Wofford *Journal*, the college's literary quarterly. "We'll make this rag the best college magazine in the South," announced the new editor, a brilliant senior from Georgia. For our world-rending first issue I contributed an incomprehensible haiku, a drawing that suggested a couple in coitus to illustrate another student's poem, "Love Song of an Athenian Eunuch," a cartoon of a student astride a toilet in Wightman Hall with a pipe leading from the commode to an awfully well drawn director of food services who held a bucket to catch the waste. *Ezra Pound rules!*

All copies of the *Journal* were confiscated by the dean of students within an hour of publication. The editorial staff was rounded up and charged with violating the Student Code of Conduct, thus bringing "scorn and opprobrium" upon the college. The editor's straight 4.0 didn't protect him from being summarily expelled. The assistant editor (top student and son of a Methodist preacher) was kicked out for two semesters. Me? I was put on "Conduct Probation" for one year—the Judicial Board reasoned that I was an impressionable sophomore who had come under the spell of two seductive seniors and didn't know what I was doing.

I knew what I was doing.

This sad episode in the intellectual history of the college is testimony to administrative paranoia in the sixties. Left-wing students burning buildings at Columbia and Berkeley, could Wofford be far behind?

"One Saturday night I vomited on the steps of the president's house, so drunk I thought I was in Snyder Hall, and they didn't put me on Conduct Probation," marveled a fraternity brother. "Makes one question the school's priorities."

Two years later, graduation weekend, Dean Logan accosted me. "I want to meet your mother. She seems a remarkable woman."

My mother?

A decade later when Wofford made me the youngest member of the board of trustees (the college doesn't hold grudges), the now defanged dean admitted, "Back when we were going to kick you out, I called your parents so they could bolster themselves for your expulsion. I told your mother that your writing was salacious, immature, and boorish. Your mother replied, 'I've always known he was immature but salaciousness is a surprise. His boorishness is undeniable. That is why I thought the cure for his deficiencies would be a good liberal arts education.'"

Dean Logan said, "I ended the call, ran across the hall and yelled at the Judicial Board, 'We're fixing to kick out a student for being ignorant, boorish, and uncouth? Damn it, that's the whole point of the college—*to civilize the little bastards!*'"

A bow-tied Yale professor (a flutist) took umbrage at my mildly critical review of his precious preaching book, threatening, "You're finished with the *Christian Century*." I countered, "If the spring '65 *Journal* didn't end my writing career, you won't."

After "The *Journal* Affair" I swore: *never again will I publish anything that I can't blame on God.*

*   *   *

A writer who professes nonchalance about audience reaction is lying; every writer must be called for by readers.

"Whatever you do, for God's sake don't ask a question. That really pisses off Holmer," advised the older, wiser graduate stu-

dent. This, my sole preparation for Paul Holmer's legendary Kierkegaard class, Yale Divinity School, fall 1969.

Sure enough, first session, after a lecture on SK's early years, in which Holmer implied that he had hobnobbed with the Melancholy Dane during his student days in nineteenth-century Copenhagen, Holmer looked out at the class and asked, "Questions?"

A pompous, widely loathed know-it-all from Ohio stood and launched a prolix, self-important interrogation, inquiring into SK's antecedents. Hume? No? Kant? Ah yes, *Goethe!*

Holmer stared at the pedant for the longest time, then looked away with disdain. "Other questions?"

He didn't teach Kierkegaard; Holmer was Kierkegaard. Master of sardonic humor and ironic wit, lover of enigmatic insight and the paradoxical phrase, every class an adventure. "Preaching does not remove the offense proffered by Christ but rather accentuates our vexation at finding God on a cross," harrumphed Holmer, channeling SK.

"If Hegel is right in what he says about the Christian faith, why did not God incarnate as a German professor rather than as a Jew from Nazareth?" SK quoted by Holmer with a smirk.

Like SK, Holmer was contemptuous of culturally relevant clergy. When students packed the Commons Room to hear Holmer debate our sixties hero, William Sloane Coffin, on the role of the pastor in come-of-age 1960s' America, Coffin opened with an overwrought exposition of the pastor as agent of social change. "You will preach to people of influence—bankers, lawyers—organize them to work for social justice. Together you can change your community!"

Holmer sniggered, "I disagree with everything Bill has said. Your job can't be to organize people, to make a 'community.'

Really now. Groups are how people hide, contemptible cowards. Community, particularly church, their best defense against God. A good pastor breaks up groups, strips people naked so God can get to them. Besides, Jesus despised bankers and lawyers, no less than clergy, organized or not."

After a proto-womanist lecture on the rise of feminist theology, in which the speaker claimed that at last women had progressed to where they could name their ecclesiastical bondage and rise above Christian benightedness, as we applauded, Holmer muttered, "By God, nobody insults my grandmother!"

For my semester paper I produced "Kierkegaard on Preachers Who Try to Be Poets," a meditation on Kierkegaard's aphorism "Truth is not nimble on its feet."

Holmer concluded the last class with "Willimon? Who is Willimon?"

I raised a trembling hand.

"Come by my office. This afternoon," said Holmer. "We must discuss your paper."

In the next hours I agonized over every footnote and cross-examined every assertion.

I'm too conceited to plagiarize and too cowardly to challenge the prejudices of the professor. What academic crime have I committed?

At three, I tapped on his office door in Beecher House. Holmer was seated at his disordered desk.

"Where did you learn to write?" he demanded.

I sheepishly admitted that I graduated from Wofford where Vince Miller taught me to read, but not to write.

"Perhaps that explains," said Holmer, gazing out the window onto the quad.

"Explains?" I asked, quiveringly.

Holmer gestured at a stack of student papers. "Sad. Uninformed, insufferably pompous. But your paper. I was brought to tears."

Tears?

"My Lord, you Southerners can write, I'll grant you. You can make an argument, and beguilingly. Perhaps you got that way defending the indefensible. You are wrong about Kierkegaard, of course, but how you made me wish you were right! You have a grand career ahead, I'm sure. What Southern preacher lets the facts stand in your way? Right? They pay good money for gifts like yours in Texas. I see a large church in your future, in Dallas. You can write."

I sailed across Sterling Quad. Paul Holmer had made me bivocational.

When I became a professor, I was thrilled that Holmer was coming to Duke to give the philosophical theology lecture. I eagerly awaited him at the hall where he was to speak. When he appeared with his hosts, I rushed up. "Professor Holmer, remember me? I was in your Kierkegaard class at YDS. Wrote a paper on Kierkegaard and preaching. You encouraged me to publish the paper. Well, I did. And maybe as a result of that class paper I'm now here, a professor of liturgy and worship at Duke Divinity."

Holmer glanced at me as he sighed. "I don't remember you."

＊　　　＊　　　＊

My friend Stanley Hauerwas says I write well because I'm an indiscriminate reader. By age ten I had read the twenty volumes of *The Book of Knowledge*, which my grandmother had bought off an Illinois peddler. At eleven I earned the swimming merit badge by teaching myself the backstroke and breaststroke, as well as the Australian crawl, by reading *The World Book.*

I came close to reaching my goal of reading all the holdings of the Greenville High School library but midway through got distracted by the Harvard Classics in the public library, where I spent many a Saturday. I built shelves around my pine-paneled room, Prospero, with magic books embracing me. To prepare for seminary, I laboriously outlined the Niebuhr brothers' works as well as Tillich's *Systematic Theology*, volumes 1 and 2, and Bultmann's *Jesus Christ and Mythology* before I knew better. When I entered Yale's Sterling Library and gazed upon the pseudo-Gothic fresco of Alma Mater blessing the circulation desk, I had the closest thing to a mystical experience that's allowed Methodists.

In his *Confessions*, Augustine claims that a pagan book, Cicero's *Hortensius*, inflamed him, shook him, and changed his life. Quite a boast for a book.

Paulo and Francesca, in Dante's *Inferno*, sit under a tree reading. Their eyes meet, and "That day we read no more." For the two young lusters, a book was a procurer luring them where they would not have gone by themselves.

Books that have been similarly inflammatory and seductive for me are by Dostoevsky (Jesus takes nobody except the broken), Flaubert (every writer must work up the gumption to write after reading *Madame Bovary*), Dante (fruit of two years of Duke Italian with a professor who knew me as Guil Guillemon), Flannery O'Connor (by comparison, I'm such a liar), Thomas Mann (three years of German to read the interminable sentences of *The Magic Mountain*), Nabokov (deeply ashamed that I was tricked into sympathy for *Lolita*'s pedophile Humbert Humbert), and Proust (four times through *Remembrance of Things Past*, guilty pleasure, none of it usable in sermons). Proust did the best job ever of "the drama of undressing" through the *mémoire involontaire*, spontaneous, unsought memory that reveals "the habitually concealed essence of things," helpful in figuring out a congregation.

Having been saved by the ministrations of a book, Christians tend to be big readers. A group of clergy told me that because I was a bad bishop for Alabama, they were conspiring to have me moved. ("You're just an academic." "You have a harsh tone in your voice." "You and your wife act like you think you're better than us." After that, their criticism got nasty.) Feelings of past rejections arose: last one picked for the softball team, sacked from the college president search, only boy without a tie. How did I recover? I stole into my basement study and read myself back into the game, digesting fifty management/leadership books my second episcopal year. If *The World Book* taught me the breaststroke, business books could make me be a better bishop. Saved by books.

As with *Winnie the Pooh*, some books should be read only at certain times in life. No sophomore needs the Song of Songs, and it's dangerous for anybody my age to traffic in Ecclesiastes. All faculty should be forced to plow through Goethe's *Faust*. Any nineteen-year-old can make love without Wordsworth. Like sexual enhancement drugs, poetry is necessary only after fifty.

Gerard Manley Hopkins famously forsook poetry and burned his poems when Cardinal Newman talked him into the Catholic priesthood. However, for a preacher in danger of flaccidity, good poetry is priesthood's partner, whipping up my imagination and flushing platitudinous verbiage. Yeats, Denise Levertov, Wal-

lace Stevens, Anne Sexton, and
Mary Oliver are calisthenics for a
preacher, enabling greater inten-
sity and concision when putting
language under pressure in the
pulpit. Caveat: A good poem demands repetition and sustained
reflection, which are ruinous in
sermons. Bad poetry, though easily accessible, exploits the moral
weaknesses of listeners. *Don't quote poetry in sermons.*

Good preachers are voracious readers, recognizing in writers
and stand-up comics our kith and kin who, like our Lord and
Dostoevsky, create worlds through words. Iced in one Saturday
in Springfield, Massachusetts, I purchased the longest, cheapest
book at the airport store. I began reading *The Brothers Kara-
mazov.* When I landed in Raleigh/Durham the next evening, as
I finished the last page and deplaned, I blinked my eyes; I was no
longer living in the world I inhabited twenty-four hours earlier.

In flawless Russian, I begged Fyodor, "Show me how to do
that to a congregation."

*   *   *

Thanks for putting up with my circuitous comedy of vocation.
Agatha Christie's Miss Marple narrates "A Christmas Tragedy,"
opening with, "I fear that I'm very inclined to ramble . . . you
must all bear with me if I tell my story badly."

I vowed to myself I wouldn't do memoir. Glad I didn't swear
on the Bible. My hesitancy to self-disclose is not because I'm
modest; it's due to my vocation. After subjection to an alleged
sermon on trust—in which the preacher went on and on about

her ever-so-funny uncle in overalls (depicted on the congregation's drop-down screen) who set dear little What's Her Name on top of the refrigerator, thus causing the child's awfully funny fall to the floor, leading the sweet little thing not to trust Uncle So-and-So for the longest time—I said to Patsy on the way home, "Thank you, and indeed all laity, for being so very interested in the personal lives of clergy! How much easier it is for preachers to talk about ourselves rather than God."

One of the joys of being a gospel preacher is that vocation is our master rather than our empathetic, all ears, sycophantic listener. Or as Karl Barth put it, "Preachers, the Bible is more interesting than you." I agree with Barth that, having so relentlessly revealing and truthfully self-communicative a God, we know more about the Trinity than we'll ever know about ourselves. As I write this memoir, Nietzsche whispers, "Self-presentation is not to be trusted." I can't be *Dragnet*'s Joe Friday, revealing "the facts ma'am, just the facts" about me, since I'd be the last to know.

In my misgivings about my ability to render an unvarnished account of me, I'm encouraged by Annie Dillard, who said to a group of writers just before publication of her memoir, *An American Childhood*, "Embark upon a memoir for the same reason that you would embark on any other book: to fashion a text. Don't hope in a memoir to preserve your memories. If you prize your memories as they are . . . avoid . . . writing a memoir. Because it is in a certain way to lose them. You can't put together a memoir without cannibalizing your own life for parts. The work batters on your memories. And it replaces them."

Gertrude Stein dismissed autobiography as inferior literature that "anyone can write," then proved herself wrong in *The Making of Americans*. Critic Roy Pascal, in his *Design and Truth in Autobiography*, charges that most memoir falls short in its "depiction of the whole personality" because of autobiographers' "lack of moral responsibility to their task." That's a bit harsh. Be suspicious of memoirists who claim to give you a fully accurate rendition of themselves. I'm under no compulsion to display my "whole personality" because, as I have already told you, the most interesting thing about me is my vocation. The me recollected by my I is limited to the me under the sway of God's call.

Autobiography is perhaps an insurmountable challenge if one respects truth. In April 1962 (the year I plodded through *The Sound and the Fury* at Greenville High) William Faulkner told a West Point class that in his youth he smuggled bootleg Cuban green rum into New Orleans for "a hundred dollars a trip." Nothing in Faulkner's story was true. Hemingway boasted that he and his impoverished lover hunted pigeons in a Paris park, living off squab for a year. "Papa" lied.

Why should I lie when I can boast of verifiable pastoral achievements like serving as the pastor of Vanna White (taciturn star of TV's *Wheel of Fortune*)? Vanna was a member of my church youth group in North Myrtle Beach and a stellar student in my annual "Sex, Dating, and Marriage like a Christian" class. Her mother was church treasurer. I would go into more detail about how my counsel shaped Vanna's Hollywood success if I were not the pastor who advised Vanna, as a high school senior, "You paid good money to go to one of those bogus modeling schools! Vanna, you're a sweet girl and we love you but let's face it, you ain't going to Hollywood. Nursing is a more appropriate career."

Vanna made more dough filming one episode of *The Wheel* than the largest annual salary paid to me for giving astute spiritual advice to youth.

I take five pages to tell of my vocation; Proust goes on for four thousand. It's a meandering journey to the end of *Remembrance of Things Past*. As the bell tolls and Maurice gazes upon the sagging paunches of his once glitterati friends, we finally figure out that Proust observed with microscopic detail and indulged in such long sentences because writing is the way to do something about death. Only writing endures.

Though Proust was right about much, he was wrong about the death-defeating powers of authorship. There's no earned immortality, even by art. Neither you nor the Lord will remember these words next week. And, by the way, the *Hortensius*—the Ciceronian treatise that made such an impact upon young Augustine? Lost forever.

In a Duke Chapel sermon on Psalm 25:7, "Remember Not the Sins of My Youth, Remember Me," Elizabeth Achtemeier recalled a self-important faculty colleague who had no time to waste with her when she was a struggling young professor; he was writing important books, and she was only a girl in a man's world.

"As he lay dying, I visited him in hospital," Betty said. "Comatose, tubes coming out of his nose. His wife had stacked his four books on the bedside table to comfort him." Betty paused for effect, tilted toward the congregation, stared them down through her granny glasses, and took her voice down to a threatening whisper. "Friends, when you die, you die, and all that you proudly created dies with you. If God forgets to take you along into eternity, *you are without hope*." Betty, kicking butt for Jesus.

When he produced his sixth volume in *Church Dogmatics*, Barth said the angels laughed, "Look! There's old Barth pushing his wheelbarrow full of such big books." Christians write, not in some vain attempt at legacy, but because, one, God is a big talker who enjoys conversation, doing some of God's best work through books, and two, we are ordered to give testimony (Luke 21:12–19), accounting for the hope that is within us (1 Pet. 3:15). Why keep good news to ourselves?

My first book was a young readers biography of the abolitionist Grimké sisters, coauthored with Patsy when she studied children's literature for her master's. After an article in *Christianity Today*, "Must We Devastate to Deliver?"—Bonhoeffer's musings on the challenge of evangelizing strong, secular, modern people—Judson Press invited me to expand the article into a book. (I didn't know then that anybody can take a random Bonhoeffer thought and work it up into a decidedly un-Bonhoefferesque thesis.) *The Gospel for the Person Who Has Everything* was a rehash of sermons in my first congregation, Trinity.

Upon my arrival as the youngest ever professor at Duke Divinity, Dean Langford told me that I must publish to be tenured. Fine with me. Professors, just like preachers, ought to show what they've got.

Worship as Pastoral Care, luring free-church Methodists into loving the liturgy, got me tenure. Stanley, coauthor of my biggest seller, *Resident Aliens*, sullied my achievement by saying that anybody who writes a book entitled *Something AS Something Else* "doesn't know what the hell he's talking about."

After *Resident Aliens*, the deluge of a book a year and, in some years (when I had time on my hands as bishop), two. I am proud of my excessively annotated *Conversations with Barth on Preaching*, heavily footnoted in a vain attempt to impress George Hunsinger and Bruce McCormack at Princeton. *How Odd of God: Chosen for the Curious Vocation of Preaching* is the closest I've come to a systematic outlay of my Barthian theological rationale, fruit of friends Keith and Brenda Brodie's encouragement. The years I spent researching *Who Lynched Willie Earle?* were a labor of love, penance for being born in segregationist Greenville.

God loves stories. You don't have to be an English major to be a Christian, but it really helps. Flannery O'Connor said "people without hope do not write novels," nor do they read them. In late life I've needed novels, when the early thrill of vocation wilts and fiction is required to propel me beyond whatever rut I'm in. When Methodists made me morose, I became the fourteen-year-old who slipped into the Greenville Public Library and read myself into the fray, then emerged to tell the world what I had read, forever the Boy Scout scribe.

Big-time novelist friends, Reynolds Price, Tom Wolfe, Harper Lee, Allan Gurganus, and my cousin, dramatist Beau Willimon, resent how metaphorically challenged clergy stifle, rather than encourage, invention. When cousin Beau Willimon's Frank Underwood spit in the face of a Jesus statue in *House of Cards*, I was embarrassed by former students who called to say, "You helped Beau write that episode, didn't you? Willimon humor is sick."

I've seen God expand Methodists' imagination, even without their reading fiction. An egregious practice of the Council of Bishops is to assign us to a "Covenant Group." I'm clueless what covenant they have in mind. Still, because we have a living God, even the council can be smacked by the incursion of the Holy Spirit. In the Berlin meeting, the bishop leading our group said, "Let's go around, okay? And share a 'God Moment.' Okay?"

Bishops bragged about their successful hip replacement or a conference youth rally that expected 100 but, praise God, drew 120. Then a bishop from Africa said, "My 'God Moment' occurred after I presided at the wedding of a fine young Methodist couple. Her mother is active in our mission work. After the wedding, as we were departing to our homes to dress for the feast, people were running back toward the church, wailing. The bride's mother had gone home and died. Dropped dead!

"In our culture, when something bad happens on the wedding day, it's a sign that God has cursed the marriage.

"I go to her house. There she is, lying across her bed. Dead! I ask the mourners to leave me with the body. I shut the door and take her hand. It is cold. 'Lord, we must have your help. She's a good Christian who is badly needed in your work. And this young couple doesn't deserve this. Lord, come to us!'

"Her hand gripped mine. Her eyes opened. I helped her up and told her to get dressed for the feast. That was a 'God Moment.'"

I could not look at the narrating African bishop because I was looking at all the North American bishops looking at their shoes.

"George, that sure beats your hip replacement!" I exclaimed. "Come on. Can any of you bishops top that?"

The convener hurriedly called for a closing prayer—"Okay?" Scurrying out of the ballroom, a bishop from Maryland, or maybe Ohio, it's hard to tell, whispered, "You don't think that really happened, do you?"

"You're calling a fellow bishop a liar?" I asked. "God never did anything that interesting to me in Alabama, darn it. Surely the Holy Spirit is needed as badly in 'Bama as in the Congo."

David Hume taught that miracles are insufficient foundation for religious faith. Okay. But miracles sure can dis-ease essentially secular, progressive church bureaucrats and transform a dull church meeting into comic opera. Okay?

Unlike anyone else, I cherish *Incorporation* and *I'm Not from Here*, my homage to Dostoevsky and De Vries. Many were offended by the happy ending of *Incorporation*; none of the gang of ecclesiastical malefactors gets what he deserves, gleefully, happily sinning without paying for it. I like to think of *Incorporation* as a quite Christian novel written in the sure and certain hope that Jesus Christ saves sinners, only sinners, especially those who make their living off Jesus.

When I sent a copy of *Incorporation* to my buddy Adam Hamilton, he wrote that he loved the novel, but "I thought Mike Slaughter was your friend. Won't Mike take offense at your obvious references to him?"

Mike wrote to say that my satire is a riot, but "I hope that Adam won't be upset by your poking fun at his megachurch. Everybody knows that your 'Rev. Simon' is Adam."

Neither Mike nor Adam is in the book. I swear.

As for my second novel, the few people who've read *I'm Not from Here* are baffled. The book, which delights in God's work, for weal and woe, among unsuspecting folk in a small Georgia town, makes more sense if you expect Jesus to smile.

Some have said of my writing, as Martin Luther scoffed after reading *Defense of the Seven Sacraments* (ascribed to Henry VIII but probably written by Thomas More), "Either a fool wrote it, or a fool let it go out under his name."

While working in the Barth archives in Basel, I saw Barth's personal copy of *Romans* in which he scribbled: "Karl Barth, to his dear Karl Barth, 1922." Below he added a quote from Luther: "If you feel that you are right and suppose that your book . . . is a great achievement . . . feel your ears. . . . You will find that you have a splendid pair of big, long, shaggy asses' ears."

When I donated copies of my eighty books, a dozen of which were translated into six languages, along with hundreds of articles, to the archives at Birmingham-Southern College, my authorial output consumed eighty feet of shelving. Why this excessive need to get my thoughts in front of everyone? You tell me. *Insecurity about my paternity? Adolescent rebellion against Methodist mediocrity? Atonement for sophomore sin? Premature toilet training?*

"Lord, you're impressed by my publishing productivity, aren't you?" I asked in prayer, after a negative review by one of the Lord's buddies. "I've received awards. Even my earliest work is still in print."

"I never felt the need to write," Jesus replied, dismissively. "Unlike you, Matthew, Mark, and Luke showed some restraint. You could profit from closer editing. And, to tell the gospel truth, in your last book you seemed to be repeating yourself."

"But don't you think that my writing has helped clarify the Christian faith for those dear souls from the Midwest who have difficulty believing?"

"Not really," replied our Lord, in love.

Maybe I've written so much because writing was easy. When a student asked, "Miss O'Connor, why do you write?" Flannery replied, "Because I'm good at it."

"His writing is good," they said of Paul, "but his public speech is nothing" (2 Cor. 10:10). Unlike Paul, if my writing is any good, it's due to my preaching. In my first tiny congregations, I preached three sermons a week, four pages each sermon. With Sunday looming, what preacher waits for poetic inspiration or succumbs to writer's block? It's your job. Preaching demystified authorship by forcing me, Trollope-like, to get in the mood to write by, one, sitting down and, two, writing.

As I moved my mother out of the rock house she had designed, I pulled *A Boy's Book of Greek Myths* off the shelf. In the flyleaf, written in pencil in a young child's hand, I read, "This book is no damn good. Robert Willimon." I was filled both with infinite desire to have known my father and deep embarrassment at my indebtedness to him.

✳   ✳   ✳

In my initial faculty review, after examining my published work during my first years at the divinity school, chair W. D. Davies said, in Welsh, but I shall translate, "This piece" (monograph on Kierkegaard in an obscure journal read by maybe a hundred professors) "is quite good. Your productivity is remarkable. Yet . . . how shall I say, much of your writing is—*popular.*"

W. D. was speechless when I thanked him in fluent Welsh, "*Diolch.*"

Eager for me to move on, my university president dismissed my writing as "journalistic," unaware of my early success in Boy Scout reportage. My paragon is Peter De Vries, who said he wanted an audience for his books large enough for his elite readers to look down upon.

During my second review, the committee warned that, though my published work was of a high level, I should take care not to be "overexposed." Who says to a preacher, "Careful! Preach only one service a week. Wouldn't want you and Jesus to be *overexposed*"?

When Duke invited me to the faculty, an editor from the *Christian Century* said, "Your writing will suffer. Few magazines want articles by professors. Academics are careful to the point of boredom, qualifying each assertion by showing they have read every book on the subject, striving not to overstate. You write like a preacher. You would rather be read than be fair, barging in, slugging the reader in the stomach, and then dashing off."

Today, the source of most autobiography is a life of pain. And there's a history of Christian memoir following the script: I was in agony due to illness (or repeated thrashings by parents, economic deprivation, racial bigotry, sexual injustice, religious persecution, or inability to live up to Mama's expectations). Then I found Jesus. Life got better. My memoir boasts little affliction (yet), terminal illness (yet), extraordinary sin (yet), hopeless addiction (yet), victimization (yet), or grave injustice (too white, too male, too privileged for that).

While my dispatches from the Boy Scout bus breakdown in Oklahoma taught me that it's sweet to wrench some modicum of meaning out of one's misfortune by writing, pain is not the teacher some autobiographers make it out to be. In *Speak, Memory*, Nabokov mocks the "idiot who, because he lost a fortune in some crash, thinks he understands me."

The best of Christian memoirists (John Bunyan, Anne Lamott, Harry Emerson Fosdick, Annie Dillard, Kathleen Norris, Eugene Peterson, Lauren Winner, Kate Bowler) claimed not that they suffered extraordinarily but rather that something undeservedly wonderful has happened to them, good news that begs to be shared. If they've had anguish, it's discipleship-induced pain akin to that portrayed in Lamin Sanneh's *Summoned from the Margin*. Jesus promised us a cross to bear, not because life can be tough but because cross is what the world does to people who follow Jesus. Jesus blessed the wounded and the victimized but never made human wounds a badge of honor or victimization a blessing in disguise. Alleviation of human pain does not seem to have been a major interest of Jesus. My losses have been little, everyman losses, not great, unjust ones. Besides, as Karl Barth said, never give evil or sin undeserved glory by touting your tragedies.

Mischief was worked in the church by Henri Nouwen's *The Wounded Healer.* I'm sure Henri did not mean that an unfortunate life necessarily qualifies a person for ordained ministry, but that's how many mistook him. Pity the poor congregation whose pastor says, "After my third divorce and sixth job change, I thought, 'Maybe the pastoral ministry would be therapeutic for one so wounded as I.'"

As early as the 1550s, Richard Hooker (book 5 of *Ecclesiastical Polity*) lamented those "forlorn men" who, "having failed at every worldly endeavor," lapse into the less demanding life of the cloth where they bed down with a hypochondriacal congregation, happy as pigs in mud.

This preacher memoirist must disappoint by having so little distress to report. Still, I'm encouraged that Natalia Ginzburg, Italian communist, claims that happiness can be the writer's friend. "When we are happy we . . . are cooler, clearer, more separate from reality." In happiness, writers are free to "look away from ourselves, we look upon others more directly, without fear, self-pity, or that self-absorption that afflicts us when we are in personal pain." Suffering impedes the writer by making "the imagination weak and lazy; it moves, but unwillingly . . . , with the weak movements of someone who is ill," making "it difficult for us to turn our eyes away from our own life."

Stephen Chapman and I taught a course on preaching from the Psalms. While some of the most moving psalms are laments, in the hands of contemporary preachers lament can be, well, lamentable. Give a mainline preacher a text like "My God, my God, why have you forsaken me?" (Ps. 22:1), and a congregational deep-dive into blathering self-pity is unavoidable.

That the average United Methodist is sixty-two is bad news for preachers; with increased age often comes greater self-absorption. (I write this at seventy-one. Can you tell?) Pity the empathetic pastor who is pummeled by aged parishioners' excessive self-concern, stoned to death with marshmallows.

Yet another gift of my vocation: My misfortunes are relativized by pastoral work. In any church I've served, there's always somebody with troubles worse than mine.

"I had a terrible accident that left me in so much pain I thought I'd go crazy," a pastor said to me. "The best therapy was to get dressed and go visit at the hospital." I knew just what she meant.

*　　　*　　　*

Though a happy peddler of words, I agree with Ignatius (in his 110 CE *Letter to the Romans* 3.3) that "Christianity is not a matter of persuasive words. Its greatness consists in its being hated by the world." Would my life have so little anguish if I had been a more cruciform practitioner of the truth that I preached? What joy to serve in Alabama, where numerous Methodist preachers had been forced to pack up the family and leave under the cover of darkness because some Alabama congregation heard the gospel articulated so well that they wanted to kill the preacher. Though I openly shared the address of my episcopal residence, the Klan saw no need to light a cross on my lawn. While I've gotten hate mail and idle threats, I've never even been fired because of what I've written. True, Jeff Sessions condemned me, and the Institute on Religion and Democracy demanded that Duke fire me, but who listens to them?

In Amsterdam, when I told Marney that I wondered how a congregation would receive me, Marney replied, "With those dimples, you will get away with heresy." Richard Hays thinks my humor makes me a moving target. Stanley says it's my "damn Southern charm," hoping one day I'll write so clearly that somebody in the Duke administration wakes up and says, "We're paying the salary of a guy who speaks against everything we believe? Are we crazy?"

The best revenge for a hard day in the classroom, my mother claimed, was in the evening to sit down at her sewing machine and create, adding something beautiful to the world, using her own hands. I'm sure that my bouts of painting, sculpting, stained-glass construction, rustic furniture creation, woodcarving, and mosaic making correlate with my hard times. What joy to join the Lord for a few hours of beating back the chaotic *tohu wa-bohu* (Gen. 1:2). When words fail, art takes up the slack. Had not God called me to be a preacher, I could have been South Carolina's Piero della Francesca. Not once but twice I've won the Duke Employee Art competition, pocketing twenty-five dollars for a batik (painted at sixteen) of a possum hanging by his tail in a persimmon tree.

When I left Duke Divinity School the first time, the bishop stuck me at Northside United Methodist Church, bragging to his buddies, "That will knock him down a notch or two. He won't be able to talk his way out of this."

"Poor Northside has set the record for attrition," said the sympathetic district superintendent. "Good luck."

Barely four hundred Methodists knocked around in a building built for two thousand. Most disheartening were the seven— count 'em, seven—empty Sunday school rooms, three of which were now used for storage, as if upon Jesus's return his first command would be "Quick. Bring me dozens of worn-out hymnals and all the rusting, folding metal chairs you can carry. Come on, people, let's inaugurate the Reign of God."

Each humiliation at Northside only validated my suspicion that that was where God wanted me. As we all know, our Savior is a sucker for lost causes.

I retaliated by commandeering one of Northside's empty classrooms, putting my books on shelves improvised from bricks and boards, and laying out ongoing writing projects on the desk. Whenever I had a free hour, I would duck into that room to read and write. Some of my friends handle their setbacks with a bottle; I do it with words.

When the idol that was communism betrayed Richard Wright (*The God That Failed*), Wright said his only hope was "to hurl words into this darkness and wait for an echo; and if an echo sounded, no matter how faintly, I would send other words . . . , to keep alive . . . the inexpressibly human."

Time and again as a hurler of words, my vocation has kept me human, moving me from tears to laughter (Matt. 5:4), but only after I submissively bowed to vocation's demands. When I was a bishop, writing rescued me from my sub-Christian desire for revenge upon my detractors and from despair over Methodism's sorry state, enabling me to lose myself in service to my calling, forever the itinerant cub reporter telling Greenville the truth about life on the way to the Jamboree, hurling words in the happy, happy, accidental life that is not my own.

*   *   *

Like every preacher, my favorite O'Connor story is "Revelation." Here's how I tell it:

Ruby Turpin sat with her taciturn husband, Claud, in a crowded doctor's waiting room. And as Ruby often did, she occupied her meager mind by going around the room one by one evaluating every person, measuring herself by those who were seated before her. As she placed herself on the social ladder, Ruby always came out more than a step above everybody else—on this occasion, particularly above that sullen-looking teenage girl seated across from her, unkempt, pockmarked, and sour. Ruby tried to make conversation with a couple of the nicer-looking people in the room. She then tried talking with the girl's mother but failed to elicit a response from the girl. The girl's name? Mary Grace.

Ruby chattered on about the importance of good posture, the value of greeting the world with a smile, and other inanities, loud enough for everyone in the waiting room to hear. She talked about the relative value of black field hands compared to "poor white trash," though you had to pay them a full day's wage. And you had to take them home at the end of the day, even though it was no more than half a mile's walk. Ruby said she knew white trash who lived in houses worse than some of "our pigs that Claud and me has got."

Ruby prattled until the unkempt, scowling teenager fixed her eyes on her, "like drills," making Ruby very uncomfortable.

Ruby squinted at the title of the girl's book—*Human Development*. She could imagine the lurid things in that book. Without warning, Mary Grace hurled the huge book across the waiting room, coldcocking Ruby across the forehead. Ruby sprawled in the middle of the floor. The girl was on top of her hissing, "Go back to hell where you came from, you old warthog."

It is the beginning of Ruby's undesired revelation. Grace, difficult grace. Before the story ends, God gives Ruby a stunning vision of universal redemption in which everyone she despises, all the "freaks and lunatics shouting and clapping and leaping like frogs," are moving upward toward paradise. And bringing up the rear are people she recognizes as those like Claud and herself, marching with dignity, always responsible for "good order and common sense," shocked to have all their virtues "being burned away." In the end, there's no hope for any of us, respectable or not, except by God's mercy, God's grace. And in the Christian faith, grace, revelation, often comes when a large book smacks you upside the head.

All I am is Mary Grace, the accidental Methodist preacher and writer. My divinely assigned task, after being personally assaulted by the gospel, is to whop 'em in the head with a book and allow God to do the rest.

8

Unanticipated Friends

Ye are my friends, if ye do whatsoever I command you. . . . I
call you not servants; for the servant knoweth not what his
lord doeth: but I have called you friends. . . . Ye have not
chosen me, but I have chosen you, and ordained you, that
ye should go and bring forth fruit. (John 15:14–16)

Four years of high school Latin rendered me impervious to academic pain. That a pea-brained NRA Republican (*a tautology*?)
wants to arm teachers shows how low the profession of second-
ary school teaching has sunk. Miss Boggs had no need of a pistol
to drive a defensive lineman to his knees, whimpering like a baby,
begging to go to the boys' restroom to blow his nose, promising
never again to screw up the conjugation of *pugnare*. In Latin IV,
Miss Boggs blessed my life (without intending to) by forcing us
to translate Cicero's *De amicitia* ("On Friendship").

Simone Weil said nothing helps us stay focused upon God
better than "friendship for the friends of God." You meet Jesus
by being introduced to him by his friends. Because I spent so

much of my childhood alone in the woods, hankering for friends, longing to be a member of a club, God inducted me, Jonah, and Jeremiah into the "great company of preachers."

If one stumbles, a friend can help him up, says Ecclesiastes. Pity the one who falls without friends (Eccles. 4:10). When I have been pushed by Jesus into some unpopular position, when I've failed to accomplish a coveted goal or am denied an accolade that I just have to have, I revert. I'm Christopher Robin in the house in the middle of the woods, alone, father absent, mother away at school, a kid in bad need of friends.

The Lord gave the word: great was the company of preachers (Ps. 68:11). How fortifying, when you are struggling to preach at twenty-six, to have a two-thousand-year consortium backing you up. Dead preachers gave me friendly formation: Augustine doling out the gospel to a sweaty congregation in North Africa; Massillon sticking it to Louis XIV; Hawley Lynn daring a sermon on lynching in Pickens, South Carolina; Bessie Parker taking a congregation of white racists to church at Indian Field UMC; Gardner Taylor picking the pockets of my congregation at Duke Chapel before they realized they had been had.

The two years I spent working with Rick Lischer on our *Concise Encyclopedia of Preaching*, calling upon hundreds of homiletical friends to cover every aspect of preaching, showed my indebtedness to friends and homage to the craft that has consumed my life.

Karl Barth, my first best preacher friend, gave me guts. On December 10, 1933, Barth preached in the *Schlosskirche* in the University of Bonn. Only about a year into Hitler's chancellorship of the Reich, the university had fallen into the hands of *der Führer* with students and faculty eagerly devising intellectual justifica-

tion for Nazi anti-Jewish laws. Barth stood in the university pulpit and, armed with Romans 15, preached on Christian kinship with God's elect, Israel.

A number of people walked out before the preacher finished. The next day Barth mailed his sermon to Hitler. Shortly thereafter Barth was ejected from his professorship and from Germany.

Sixty years later I preached from that pulpit in Bonn (nobody walked) and lectured in the same hall (few attended) where Barth held his homiletics class while Nazis monitored from the rear of the room.

"I didn't know that Herr Hitler had an interest in preaching," Barth quipped jovially.

Hardly a week goes by that I've not called upon Barth for aid. Never has he failed to help with heavy lifting.

*   *   *

Stuck at failing Northside, I received a letter from Stanley Hauerwas, then of Notre Dame, praising my baptism book. Having just read Stanley's dissertation on Wesley, Calvin, and sanctification, I posted his letter in the boiler room where I, at 6:30 a.m., on cold Sundays, was delegated to light a candle to ignite the burner of the church's aging boiler, and took heart that somewhere an honest-to-God intellectual liked me.

Proust said that friendship is the lie that we tell ourselves to deceive ourselves that we are not alone. I say that friends, wisely chosen, aid us not only in self-deceit but also in pursuit of self-truth. After a clever chapel sermon, pleased with my efforts, postservice, receiving fawning fans, Savonarola—still stinking from incineration for his Florentine tirades—looked down from his niche and sneered, "You compromised twit. If you had preached truth, they would be less grateful."

What Methodist church puts statues at the door to mock the preacher?

My listeners are in trouble when it comes to hearing the voice of God. To batter their inexhaustible defenses I summon homiletical colleagues. Preachers improve through imitation, apprenticeship to an experienced colleague. As a young preacher I arose early on Sundays, found *The Protestant Hour*, and thrilled to Edmund Steimle ladling out Lutheran gospel in tough, Yankee brogue. Grace, running naked through the streets. Holding my cassette recorder to the radio, I captured Steimle's sermon, then replayed it a dozen times the following week, making his sermon mine. I met Steimle only once—in the small men's room of the Union Seminary library where he awkwardly received my acknowledgment of homiletical indebtedness.

My first month at Yale, William Sloane Coffin began a sermon, "Of all the pornographic books ever written, none is as dirty as one minute in the mind of General William Westmoreland." How did Coffin know a Spartanburg native so well? I was hooked.

During another Battell Chapel sermon, a young man suddenly stood up and screamed, "That man is an apostate! He is preaching lies! Lies!"

Coffin didn't miss a beat. "Son," he jovially called to him across the church, "you could be right. But, come on. At least wait to make your judgment about my preaching until I get to the end of my sermon. May I finish?"

"Sure," said the young man. He sat quietly through the rest of the sermon and service.

I want to be that preacher when I grow up.

"Atta boy, treat 'em rough!" Coffin praised my Riverside sermon a decade later.

"Thanks, I owe it to you." Elisha gratefully receiving Elijah's mantle.

Courage in a preacher is the fruit of peer pressure. I read everything by Marney and, as I drove about town visiting at the hospital or stalked an errant parishioner, I listened to his sermons. I wrote Marney's obituary for the *Christian Century*, quoting, "Most preachers lack enough confidence in the gospel to damn a church mouse."

Sermons are public art, addressed to a group, arising out of a community, therefore every sermon trades in friendship—a preacher who has been cornered by Jesus, with dozens of intended listeners crowding the study joining the Holy Spirit in encouragement. An unindebted preacher is a poor preacher, though the line between grateful apprenticeship and smarmy plagiarism gets thin.

Years ago somebody published a collection of women's sermons. After a preface arguing that women preach in a way that is quite special, very perceptive, even unavailable to men, the book's first sermon was one that a woman on the West Coast had purloined from me! A cute piece on John 3 that I had preached a few years before at Duke Chapel. When I complained to Stanley, he replied, "By God, you *do* preach like a woman!" My own incriminating paper trail is too long for me to be righteously indignant that a fellow preacher snitched one of mine.

At Duke Divinity I assign students to teams of three because preachers accomplish little on their own. The students hate these triads, complaining that their group is "not a good fit."

"Welcome to Christian ministry," I respond. "You'll spend the rest of your life dependent upon people you don't like."

Wesley intended Methodist preachers to be a preacher club. For eight years I was privileged to be an overseer of six hundred clergy. United Methodists may be squeamish on the authority of Scripture or the reality of resurrection, but we unite in our conviction that clergy ought to never, ever be left alone.

Indeed, in *Bishop: The Art of Questioning Authority by an Authority in Question*, I testified to how much I owed to the Bishop's Cabinet—a dozen district superintendents who made me better than if I had tried to be bishop without friends. Still, Nietzsche charged that systems of domination take many forms, one of which is friendship.

"You'll know you're a bishop," warned Dean Greg Jones, "when you tell a joke and everybody around the table laughs too loud and too long."

I'm embarrassed that my best training to be an episcopal leader came not from being a student at Yale Divinity but as officer of Pi Kappa Alpha. In planning parties and extracting dues from sociopathic, alcohol-besotted Pikes, one gains leadership skills that last a lifetime. A fraternity is about friendship; coercing you to refer to one another as "brother," just like oldtime Methodists. Thus the fraternity was, before ordination, my most intense experience of friendship, partying, forbearing, and building a homecoming float with those who are at their best liquored up on Saturday nights, backed up by a beachmusic band.

"The US Army created college fraternities to prepare young men for platoons because, let's face it, nobody wants to die for the United States, but everybody acts brave in front of their buddies," declared a speaker at an antiwar rally in the sixties. Maybe that's why Jesus made us his friends and sent us out two by two (Mark 6:7). Who volunteers to die for an abstraction like The Methodist Church, Inc., diversity, multiculturalism, or generous orthodoxy? So Jesus made us his friends who would rather stomach the world's wrath than disappoint him.

*   *   *

I can come up with all sorts of noble reasons why I ran for bishop, but to be honest, I'm sure that a major appeal of the episcopacy was once more to risk the climb to the top of the barn, to push back the tin roof so that I could see all the way to the mountains. The opportunity to be at the top in order to lead the corporate embodiment of concepts, to move beyond slogans to performance, to solve communal problems in concert with others is the toughest intellectual work I've done. "Leadership is the art of influencing people through words," said one of my management books; *that is, preachers ought to run the world.*

As good as words are, there is no way to talk people into undertaking painful work that they've been avoiding for decades without becoming friends. Episcopal election required a year touring the Southeast, tap dancing before every caucus and conventicle, trying to find the right words to talk the church into facing the facts they had denied. When I groused about the grueling episcopal beauty pageant, a teenager explained, "We got to see if we like you enough to follow you."

Friendship all the way down.

Eleven o'clock Saturday night, attending a "Jesus rave" at one of my churches in a dilapidated warehouse, watching a boodle of mean-looking teenagers gyrating to acid-rock Jesus music, I shouted to the prim young woman in charge, "Er, uh, how did you get into this ministry?"

She yelled over the thunderous percussion: "I wanted to work with college students, but these were the only ones Jesus gave me."

In ministry, we go with the friends God sends and make the best of it.

The next morning, same church—bleary-eyed and head aching—I was the helpless prey of some horrible country western Jesus music. The pastor whispered, "We're going to show a short video just before you speak."

Anything to stop that guy from twanging.

"Why I Love Innerchange Church" was the video's theme. A young woman holding a small child testified, "My boyfriend beat me up so bad I couldn't leave the trailer. The baby needed milk so I put on makeup and dark glasses and went to the store. In the produce section, this woman come up and asked, 'Who put them marks on you, honey?' I told her I had a car wreck. She said, 'A man did that! I been through it, honey, so I know. You need friends in the worst kinda way. I'm taking you to church.' I didn't know what 'church' was. She picked me up the next morning, and once I got here I said to myself, 'This is the family God meant me to have.'"

I sailed back to Birmingham in my bishopmobile, 90 miles an hour, shouting to the disbelieving world, "*Methodism ain't dead yet!*"

*　　　*　　　*

Never a truer word was spoken by my mother than "Without Patsy, you would be a disaster." Bernard of Clairvaux made monastic celibacy so appealing that, when he preached, "Mothers hid their sons, women shut up their husbands." It surprises me that so good a preacher as Bernard had so low an opinion of matrimony. Not that he cares, but I wish our Lord had not demanded that his disciples abandon their families in order to "Follow me."

In Patsy's family, the Methodist church was like the US government for the Clintons. Patsy's father, grandfather, and *grandmother* (legendary Bessie Parker, first ordained woman in South Carolina

Methodism, 1956) were preachers. After a career in accounting, even without theological training, Patsy's older brother Fred was assigned two churches; gospel preaching is what Parkers do.

Although we married for love, who knows if part of Patsy's lure, beginning in high school—when my eyes first fell upon her in an irresistible, tight, powder blue sweater, circle pin, and Bass Weejuns—was that I inchoately knew that she knew more than I about what God was pushing me into?

Since, "I love you" often means "I love me and want to use you to love me even more," ambitious people do well to test our declarations of love by Aristotle's canon: true friends don't just love one another but love the same good things in the same way. It's great to have someone bodily present who understands, down deep, the peculiar demands of this vocation and helps concoct excuses for poor sermons.

Because deceit is the death of preachers (and people do a lot of lying to pastors), it's salubrious to snuggle, on a cold, dark night, close to a friend who knows me well and doesn't mind telling the truth.

I wish I had as good a title for my memoir as my friend Kate Bowler's *Everything Happens for a Reason and Other Lies I've Loved.* Throughout my ministry, I've told a few whoppers and embraced some doozers of deceit. On the way home after service in Duke Chapel, Patsy said casually, "I would be interested—indeed, much of the congregation would like to know—what possessed you to use that concluding illustration."

"Too much?" I asked.

"Inappropriate, gratuitously crude, even," she said, in love.

Only she who has promised to stick with the preacher "for better, for worse" has the right to tell such painful truth.

Charming pastors are tempted to lead with an ingratiating personality rather than a truthful one. Self-knowledge gained by confession, forgiveness, and repentance—sometimes on Ash Wednesday in a church, at other times in an argument in a kitchen—beats an MDiv degree.

In the friendship called marriage, the same friend who cuddles next to you (Eccles. 4:11) can also knock you off a perch that's too high for your abilities. Luther called his wife, Katarina, "my chain" (Latin: *catena*. See, Miss Boggs? I was paying attention in Latin II after all). Patsy keeps my feet on *terra firma* in spite of whatever spiritual or occupational ladder I'm attempting to ascend.

*   *   *

When we married, I thought "forsaking all others and keeping only unto her as long as you both shall live" would be a full-time job. Men are hardwired, through millions of years of evolution, to mate with dozens of women in order to ensure the continuance of the race. Infidelity comes naturally.

Soon into marriage, in keeping the promise of fidelity forced upon me by submission to the strictures of the Service of Holy Matrimony, one day I wake up and I'm not trying to be faithful; faithful is who I am. I became who God promised I would be by simply keeping a vow made "before God and this company."

In Aristotelian thought, an "accident" denotes properties that are not essential to a thing's nature. A chair is a chair whether it's made of wood or metal; the material makeup of the chair is unessential to its being a chair. Material properties are accidental to essential chairness. As a male, adultery is my essential nature; fidelity is an "accident." The Christian faith is wary of essentialism. Since God's love comes to me, meets me from without, the

Christian life consists of long-term formation whereby all those virtues that God has imposed upon me become essential to who I am. Because fidelity is an acquired disposition, the celebrant asks not "Susie, do you love Skippy?" Rather, it's "Susie, *will* you love . . ." By keeping accidental promises we become who God essentially means us to be.

Even though Jesus and Saint Paul didn't think much of marriage, I've found that if a person promises to stay with you, "for better, for worse," no matter what, you come closer to understanding God's covenantal love in Christ. Or as Paul put it (Eph. 5:25), church is God loving us in the intimate way that a husband and wife love one another in bed—a sentiment I would never risk in a sermon.

The church traditionally said the best reason for marriage is support of one's vocation to discipleship. Marriage is symbiotic on vocation, commitment to something better than marriage. Preachers often lament that ministry is tough on marriage and family. Here's countertestimony. In officiating in marriages, one comes to believe the words, the words begin to describe you. Same-sex marriage? Being in the fidelity-promoting, promise-keeping, forgiveness-receiving business, the church, you'd think, would be eager to find one more occasion to make people make promises, welcoming anyone who dared to put his or her life at the mercy of the future with another human being. Go figure.

*   *   *

Because Methodist preachers (in imitation of the perichoretic Trinity) move around a lot, we have great need of supportive friends. The first Methodist bishop, Francis Asbury, opened Annual Conference by asking preachers, "Will you be traveling this year?" They had better answer, "Yes, bishop" or risk suffering the most dreaded punishment—*location.* "Located," they stayed put and, as far as Asbury was concerned, left the party. Or as Will Rogers said of Methodist itinerancy, "Methodist preachers are like manure. Spread 'em around, they do a lot of good. Pile 'em up in one place, they get to stinking."

Methodist itinerancy kept our marriage vital and our ministry in motion. In February 1974, Legrand Moody—my district superintendent who didn't like me because he was an ex-Marine—summoned me to his office. Legrand began our consultation, "Boy, didn't I tell you to get a haircut?"

"Yessir. I did."

"Humph," he said, shaking his head. "I'll get to the point. We've got a church, Trinity, in trouble down in North Myrtle Beach. Preacher left on Christmas Eve. Vaporized."

I recalled the absconding preacher from college days, the only Wofford student who bragged of practicing "Maryolatry" in his dorm room, where he offered novenas to the Virgin, with candles and incense. *Trinity must be one lousy church for the bishop to dump upon them a pastor that crazy.*

"George Baker, retired navy chaplain, good preacher but hard to get along with, has been trying to hold things together. At last George has got the attention of the bishop. They've lost four young families in the last month. George says that we've got to get somebody down there to turn it around.

"You think a lot of yourself. Well, we're going to find out just how smart you are. You are going to Trinity. Every preacher since Jack Meadors hated it, but if you work hard, keep your head down, and try to survive, we won't forget you. If you think the salary is small, wait till you see the bedroom in that parsonage! Maybe you can wring more out of 'em next year."

"Gosh, I thought I might have a couple more years at Broad Street," I managed. "At least you are telling me now, so Patsy can warn her principal that we'll be moving in June."

"Boy, have you listened to nothing I've said?" he said, smacking the Bible on his desk. "I told you this church is in trouble. You linger until June, there'll be no church there, no there there, as John Wesley said. You're moving next week."

Gertrude Stein said that.

"But, but Patsy's teaching in Clinton," I protested.

"You need to stop hanging around in my office and get right back to Clinton to tell her about the move, don't you?"

I raged until sometime just before midnight when Patsy said, "Weren't you the one who thought God wanted to use you? Looks like you are about to be used."

Patsy's father had founded Trinity thirty years before, placing Trinity's first building on the cheapest land at the beach—a swamp where local taverns dumped empty beer cans. I had heard Mr. Parker brag that he worked up those beer cans in the swamp into a great illustration for Trinity's dedicatory sermon.

We moved the next week, too young and inexperienced to know that we owed Bishop Tullis and Superintendent Moody a debt of gratitude for restoring the adventure of marriage and ministry.

"You need to thank Preacher Baker for what he's done for you here," said Trinity's lay leader, the indomitable Peggy Hursey, as she welcomed me. "He's been a friend to you."

"How would you characterize Mr. Baker's leadership in these last months?" I asked Peggy.

"He told six or seven people to go to hell who no preacher had been man enough to tell where to get off. Now this church is ready to rock and roll," she replied.

As he gathered his books, George advised, "Always do scales on the piano first thing on Sundays before you preach. Helps develop vocal range. With your scratchy voice, you need that. One more thing, son: this crowd loves to fight. Bunch of Philistines. Keep 'em fighting the devil or they'll turn and kill you!"

"How do I do that?" I asked in a trembling voice.

"Find out where Satan is in this town and then turn 'em loose."

Less than two months later, after a group of United Methodist women observed police brutality at the local jail, I preached a sermon about the evils of corrupt law enforcement, citing our Lord as a noteworthy victim. Fighting back tears, I said, "Two of our saints, Eleanor and Mary, this week engaging in their ministry at the jail, observed a policeman roughing up a young man in a back cell. When they complained to the chief, he actually said to these two saintly women" (eyes filled with tears, hardly able to speak), "'You church ladies look after your church stuff and I'll look after the jail.'"

Congregational gasp. Someone on the third pew shouts, "Busby's got two boats and an Eldorado on a cop's salary?"

"And a riding lawnmower!" added another.

I fully expected them to begin furiously tossing *Methodist Hymnals.*

"Now I can't speak for you," I continued, barely regaining my composure, "but I for one find it hard to sit back and let our church, and these dear women, be insulted by a questionable cop."

During the pandemonium I gave an altar call for anyone Jesus had summoned to aid him against cops gone bad and turned 'em loose.

*　　　*　　　*

There's no such thing as instant friends, which is why the Service of Marriage is in future tense. It's not "John, do you (or have you previously found the opportunity to) love Susan?" It's "*Will* you love . . . ?" Promises propel into the future, putting one at the mercy of the vicissitudes of another's life with little backup but a promise. Love as the fruit of marriage rather than (as most couples suppose) the cause is church wonderfully weird.

Bogus friendships are friendships of use or of pleasure, says Aristotle. Ersatz friendships end when friends no longer have use for one another or no longer get off on the same pleasures. Fortuitously, Patsy loves both me and good preaching.

Don't attempt friendship, in marriage or otherwise, without a God who forgives. If you repeatedly forgive and receive forgiveness from your lover who is, at times, your adversary (who knows the truth about you and can stick it to you anytime she pleases), it's easier to forgive enemies and to pray for those who persecute you (Matt. 5:44) while shaking hands at the church door after service.

Jesus linked friendship with discipleship: "You are my friends if you do what I command you. I do not call you servants any longer . . . ; but I have called you friends. . . . You did not choose me but I chose you. And I appointed you to go and bear fruit, fruit that will last" (John 15:14–16 NRSV). Bothered by the conditional qualifier "if," I am reminded that only a friend commands, "Come help me load the refrigerator into the van," and you obey.

The church makes couples promise to stay married "until death do us part." Strange to bring up death when most couples I marry look like they're in pretty good shape. Death intrudes into the service of marriage because the promises of marriage are one way of dealing with our temporality, clinch-fistedly saying to the future, "Take from me what you will, by God I'll still be faithful to this person." When we promise to love the unfathomable mystery that is another "for better, for worse, for richer, for poorer, in sickness and in health," we creatively deal with our radical contingency, promising constancy even amid the ravages of time.

"The truth about life is that we shall die," said writer Philip Roth, just before he died. Death is as out of control as life can get. In my years of pastoral undertaking, I have, with Hermes, served as *psychopompos*, helping some five hundred souls to the grave, privileged to say a few words in God's behalf at their end. And one approaching day my remains shall be deposited with Patsy's in the crypt of Duke Chapel, under, rather than in, the pulpit.

Augustine said, in a sermon, that as a doctor looks at a sick man in his deathbed, shakes his head and says, "He won't get out of this alive," one could look into our crib and say, "He won't get over this." As T. S. Eliot wrote in "East Coker," in *Four Quartets*, a book I requested as a gift at my high school graduation:

> In my beginning is my end. . . .
> Houses rise and fall, crumble, . . .
> Are removed, destroyed . . . in their place
> . . . a factory, or a by-pass.

We should love the church, said Eliot, as the only institution with the backbone to tell us of "sin and death and other unpleasant facts of life."

Forced by my vocation to do so much undertaking, I found that mortality was my close companion. First Dante and then Eliot were surprised that "death had undone so many." I'm not. On more than one night I've dreamed about the people I've buried—the babe whose first breath was her last, the teenager who decapitated himself in the rec room with his shotgun (and whose mother insisted that only I could perform postmortem cleanup, which was an appropriate way for me to prepare for my Good Friday sermon that very evening). Then there was the bank president who ebbed away clutching my hand, gasping, "How do I know? Tell me!" I helped each get on the bus that takes them for free to Hamlet's "undiscovered land" from which "no traveler returns."

Oh my perverse glee, at Ash Wednesday services in the chapel, to stand before a well-built nineteen-year-old Duke male—with bulging biceps and everything working—smearing a cross of ash upon his forehead. *Pulvis es et in pulverem reverteris.* Quite a rush to preach finitude to those who believe that maybe—with regular workouts and avoidance of fructose—they are immortal.

"Of course Christianity is life," says Kierkegaard. "But first it passes through death."

Vocation is an even better death-coping device than friendship. Jean Vanier, founder of L'Arche, says that all true Christian community requires "the death of the ego," which is possible only if self-loss "is our response to a call from God." Renouncing control and letting God have God's way with us in death come easier if we have practiced dying through dozens of surrenders required by "Here I am, send me."

At the foot of Benjamin Wofford's tombstone, relinquishing the success I was bred to achieve, came a dying that fit me for rejection by my college's presidential search committee, preparation for the public death inflicted by a congregation when a sermon joke goes flat, dress rehearsal for entombment in the basement of Duke Chapel, dead dog at the bottom of an abandoned well, prelude to recall by God.

Upon return to Durham after our Alabama sojourn, God allowed us to buy a house without informing us that just down the street lived UNC professional public atheist Bart Ehrman. God's justice is rough on incorrigibles like me.

Bart had made a splash with *God's Problem*. God's intellectual failing, according to Bart, is God's inability to come up with a satisfying theodicy. How can a sophisticated, University of North Carolina–chaired professor worship a God who can't explain the world's pain and suffering? (James Cone once told me that white scholars are preoccupied with theodicy because whites would rather impugn God's justice than admit the injustice inflicted by white Christians upon black Christians.)

The reason I wrote my nastiest review ever of Bart's bathetic *God's Problem* was I read Bart's book just after being at the bedside of a dying Methodist preacher.

"How are you feeling about the end?" I asked the old parson.

He replied, "Don't take this personally, but you bishops have appointed me to the crummiest congregations in this conference. I went kicking and screaming. But after a few Sundays, I grew to love the people I intended to despise. The Lord always set right what the bishop messed up. So once again, I'm being appointed a place I don't want to go. I hope that the Lord will be as good to me in this last move as in the past, waiting on me, as usual, Lord, there before I arrive."

United Methodist itinerancy gives one so much practice in being out of control that when it comes time to suffer and die, death seems like just another bad idea by a bishop that God must somehow set right.

BTW: Bart is Durham urban ministries' most generous supporter, proving that I didn't know what I was talking about when I declared, "No atheist ever funded a soup kitchen."

*   *   *

A member of my first congregation asked me to assist at the funeral of her cousin, or her aunt's plumber—who can remember? The service was in a little country church of another denomination. The preacher's voice knew only one volume—full on.

"Joe had big plans!" he shrieked. "Kept saying that one day he would straighten up! Some day he would get right with God. Well . . ." (long rhetorical pause as he looks toward the body in the casket, then cranks it up a decibel) *"it's too late for Joe! He's dead!"* (The widow begins to keen.) "But it's not too late for you!

Joe's dead!" (The preacher stamps up and down the church's aisle.) "Too late for Joe but not too late for you! And you!" (He shoves his finger at various people.) "Now's the day of decision. You better think where you'll spend eternity! You think it's hot in Georgia?" With other such exhortations he comforted them.

On the way home I said indignantly, "That was the most manipulative, insensitive excuse for a sermon I've ever heard. Can you believe that jerk?"

Patsy agreed: the preacher's tirade was unscrupulous, calloused, and inconsiderate. "Worst of all, what he said was *true*."

I've come to respect death's implacability. The neo-Gothic grandeur of Duke's West Campus was tarnished the day in 1999 friend Charles Putman died. After leading the university's farewell to Keith Brodie in 2016, in my heart I said good-bye to Duke. We bring little into this life and take nothing out. I've stood in Duke Gardens with a plastic bag in hand, attempting to sprinkle the ashes of a prominent professor in a reverent way—little remains but dust on my black shoes.

One of my favorite photos of my namesake, Will, is of the two of us, his second summer of life, on Will's first trip to the South Carolina coast. I'm leading into the surf at sunset one who only recently had learned to walk. I expected him to be afraid at his first meeting of the sea. He is no fear and all joy. He holds my hand. In the photo, you can see only our backs, an old man stooping toward the child, the child eagerly pushing forward. You can't see, but I'll never forget, the smile on his face, Will's delight as he eagerly entered the waves at my encouraging "Jump!"

I love that photo's depiction of one of the great joys of aging—leading a little one toward the grand adventure of the wide

world, gripping his hand reassuringly, egging him on to face into the wind and to leap the waves.

But yesterday, when I looked at that picture of the two of us—the little boy and the old man—it occurred to me that I had misread that moment. I, who always thought I was leading the child, saw that I was being led. Here at sunset, the sea, the vast eternity of time that was rushing toward him with promise, was ebbing away from me, taking from me all that I loved, including the little boy named for me.

He was all future; I was now mostly past. In truth, the little one, still fresh in the world, had me by the hand, encouraging me to make my way into the deep, departing. He begins life eagerly jumping forward. I clutch his tiny hand tightly, my last grasp of the future, at the end of day as I stagger uncertainly, unwillingly toward the engulfing, eternal sea. Not long from now, he'll have to let go and venture on without me. His grip is not tight enough to rescue me from the encroaching dark, the inundating deep.

No cure for that but God.

* * *

One afternoon I came upon an undergraduate in the chapel vestry, staring dumbly before the portraits of past deans of the chapel.

"That is Dean James Cleland," I instructed. "Most beloved of my predecessors. I shall outlast even his tenure."

"Odd," the student replied, pointing to the brass label on the frame. "Says here it's Franklin Hickman."

What? Some vandal had switched the labels. Maybe for years, people had been calling dead deans by wrong names!

So when I left the chapel to be bishop in Alabama, President Brodhead asked, "I suppose you will be expecting us to pay for your portrait?"

"Don't bother," I replied. "If a portrait gained some shred of immortality, it would be worth the investment. They've got the wrong names on the portraits downstairs and nobody cares. When I'm dead, portrait or no portrait, I'm dead."

But what if the deceased was a good writer? Grieving his friend Arthur Hallam, Tennyson (*In Memoriam*) describes how he sat under a tree but, unlike the Romantics, received no consolation from nature. Then, reading Hallam's "noble letters of the dead," Tennyson found in "those fallen leaves which kept their green" something that endures.

Nice try, poetic pagan. The writing left by the dead does not make up for their dying. Thus I steadfastly refused to quote Tennyson's "Crossing the Bar" at a funeral, even when the family were tithers. No matter how good his writing, Hallam's still dead.

In "The Snows of Kilimanjaro," Hemingway describes the suicide of one writer's vocation: "He had destroyed his talent himself—by not using it, by betraying of himself and what he believed in, by drinking so much that he blunted the edge of his perceptions, by laziness, by sloth, by snobbery, . . . selling vitality . . . for security, for comfort." As a bishop who severed a number of clergy from their ordination, I believe that if life really begins with being called, betrayal of vocation is deadly.

Nevertheless, as Christians, we are not allowed to give death more respect than death deserves. Our hope in death is the same as in life: the vocative, comedic God who has so vigorously called and deployed us will recall us even in death.

Dozens of United Methodist churches died on my episcopal watch; hundreds more barely had a pulse. There is little theological justification for a shrinking congregation; dwindling congregations are an affront to the God of the living and not the dead (Mark 12:26–27). Patsy and I were never appointed to a growing congregation; in more than one, the death rattle overpowered the hymns on our first Sunday. Yet we never left a congregation that was not welcoming new life. Even during our one-year interim at flagging Duke Memorial UMC, fifty-two people became members.

Church growth isn't proof that I'm Methodism's greatest evangelist. Rather, it is confirmation that Jesus Christ loves to see things grow (his parables of seedtime and harvest) and that a pastor must be a truth-teller rather than a death-denier. As Abraham Kuyper taught us, Jesus is adamant that no person, no corner of creation, fail to hear "*Mine!*"

When I proposed sending one of my pastors to remotest Alabama, he protested to the district superintendent, "That church has been dying for twenty years! It should have been closed long ago if we had competent bishops. I can't go to that church. It's dead!"

The D.S. replied, "Well, I'll tell the bishop that you don't want to go, even if you vowed to go where he sends you. But let me warn you. This new bishop believes in the bodily resurrection of Jesus. So if you say, 'That church is nothing but a stinking corpse,' it don't mean nothin' to the bishop. Just another opportunity to test Jesus's boast about being resurrection and life."

*   *   *

Homer believed that progeny is the best hedge against oblivion in Hades. No, even children as lovable as mine are unequal to the annihilation of my dying. Call me crazy, but I think a better Christian reason for bearing children into the world is preaching. Look it up: "One generation shall praise thy works to another, and shall declare thy mighty acts" (Ps. 145:4).

My absentee father made me eager to be present to my children. Parenting, as exercise of deep, complicated friendship, is obedience to Jesus's command to receive the stranger. To test our obedience to Jesus's command, the Lord calls some of us to marriage, and if you get good at receiving Christ in the presence of the stranger who sleeps next to you, the Lord may further test your receptivity to strangers by granting you children, all to train for being welcomed by the ultimate stranger, Christ (Matt. 25:30–46).

"I must talk with you," said the staid older woman who taught the Northside first grade Sunday school class.

"But the service begins in five minutes," I protested.

"Reading to the children about our Lord's nativity," she continued unabated, "I was interrupted by your son.

"He said, 'I've asked my dad how babies are made and he never said anything like that story,' upsetting our more sensitive children. Surely you would not want this whispered about in the congregation. You will know how to discipline him."

We give life to children and then they return the favor by re-birthing us parents. I've met lots of people; Harriet and William remain two of the most interesting. They are not appendages of me; they are gifts God sent for my sanctification. They in turn introduced us to equally interesting Garrett and Elizabeth. They are better parents of treasures Will, Wesley, Parker, and Grace than I was father to them. Were I not rigorously opposed to preachers who reference their family in sermons, I would say more.

Parents introduce their children to reality (i.e., God), yet in a manner whereby they are not blown away by the truth. Patsy is a master in affirming our children without creating in them undue self-deceit about God, themselves, or the world. Her capacity to be truthful, even with our children, is a gift of her Parker spiritual heritage. A father, grandfather, and grandmother who made their living telling the truth from a pulpit aided Patsy's ministry of truth telling to me and our offspring. Patsy knew how to make children and grandchildren who are committed, continuing Christians, none of whom would define the gospel as "accept your acceptance," much less dismantle Christmas decorations before Epiphany.

The younger generation helps their jaded elders rediscover the adventure of Jesus. As a child, I loved the story of the call of little Samuel when he was in service to old Eli (1 Sam. 3). I thrilled that God came to the inexperienced kid, awakening him in the middle of the night with "Samuel, Samuel . . ." rather than disturbing the sleep of the theologically trained, lifetime priest. At some point, say, the summer I became fifty-one, I resented this story. *Why would God give revelation to the untrained kid that God withheld from the aging priest?*

As I see my children and grandchildren answer when God calls their names and take their place in the pageant of Christianity (even as God takes me out), I think, *Isn't that just like the God who called little Samuel?*

In the calling of Samuel, old Eli still had to be Samuel's Marney and say, "Sounds suspiciously like God. Next time you hear your name called, say, 'Here am I.'"

Even in our dotage, there is still something we patriarchs can do for the kids.

"Papa," said Wesley Garrett Putman as he helped me put my books on the shelves of my new, and last, office. "If Duke is so happy to have you back, how come they gave you a lousy office with no window?"

If the dean can't fool a five-year-old, who can he fool? Me.

Parents preach to their progeny, but one of the challenges of Christian parenting is receiving sermons by one's children. As I sat with Wesley listening to a sermon—my favorite location to receive another preacher's product—Wesley, then age seven, nudged. I ignored him. He poked again.

"Papa," he whispered, "what does Humpty Dumpty have to do with Epiphany?" Like Psalm 145 says (in rough translation), "One generation shall make their elders uneasy by praising God in a higher key than their parents."

"Would it kill you to include just one reference to football? Maybe that's why you're preaching in North Carolina rather than northern California," suggested William.

At breakfast one morning, Patsy told the children, "Daddy is leaving for Oregon today to speak."

"Someone out there knows Daddy?" wondered Harriet, age five.

"Yes," said Patsy. "Daddy goes all over the world to tell people about God."

Harriet responded, "I hope he tells them more than he tells us." *Children.*

"Do you know what your daughter whispered to me right after your sermon?" said Tuck Jones when she and Bishop Bevel ("Bev") Jones were at lunch with us one Sunday. I froze.

"'Do you believe this?'"

"'How do you mean?' I asked."

"Harriet whispered, 'I live with him, and none of these stories really happened to him.'"

Tuck Jones replied, "Yes, dear, I too live with a preacher."

A subspecies of the genus friendship is teaching, like Paul with Timothy, or Marney with me—one generation handing over what it's learned to another. Closely allied with the arts of parenting, teaching has been ancillary to my preaching. When a student grouses, "That was more sermon than lecture," I, who disbelieve in any rigid separation of *kērygma* from *didachē*, say, "Thanks."

The guest preacher in Duke Chapel last Sunday demonstrated that anybody can give a lecture; it takes a called preacher to perform the death-defying high-wire act called preaching.

*　　　*　　　*

The first Sunday after Epiphany, 1976, Trinity UMC, North Myrtle Beach. I was greeting well-wishers and naysayers, and a couple of visitors said, "We enjoyed the service. Bob and Betty Wilson from Durham. Could we take you and your wife to lunch?"

Once we were served, Bob said, "We've been searching for a professor of worship. A student told us about you. Read your Emory dissertation. Now that I've seen you in action, we'd like to invite you to Duke. Check us out, maybe give a lecture or two."

I called Marney and asked him if I should interview at Duke. "Sure. But if you're hired by Duke, you must become more adept in using a word: *bullshit*."

We came, I lectured, they hired. Assistant Professor of

Liturgy and Worship. Back then the divinity school knew how to make a hire; trusting students to nominate, snooping around, certifying that a prospective professor actually knew how to preach before hiring to teach. I'm grateful that Duke is intellectually secure enough, open-minded enough, to have allowed me to run loose on campus for decades. Few universities and seminaries would.

At the end of my first week of classes, a student from Ohio said, "That was amazing. When I heard your hillbilly accent, I thought, *Has Duke lost its mind, hiring a person who talks like that?* But you are brilliant."

"Ms. Albert, pray to God that I'm Christian enough to forgive that remark."

"But I meant that as a compliment," she protested.

"Then pray that I'm compassionate enough not to hold your stupidity against you."

Students.

A student anonymously evaluated my missions class—to which I give 150 percent—as "story time with Will." My dragnet for that student continues.

When I brag that I'm the longest-tenured faculty member still teaching at the divinity school, Rick Lischer always jumps in with "The operative phrase is 'continuous service.' Remember? You got mad and left two or three times, and when things didn't work out where you were, we were good enough to take you back."

As I say, I'm grateful for Duke's charity.

A score of seminaries subject their charges to *Pastor: The Theology and Practice of Ordained Ministry.* During my last days at Duke Divinity, almost weekly Jesus says to me, "I'm sending you all the people you need to turn Methodism around. Try not to be so boring that we lose them to hip but tacky nondenom megachurches. Is that too much to ask?"

My organization of student mission trips to Haiti and Honduras was chiefly pedagogical. Our slogan: You can't change Honduras in a couple of weeks, but Honduras can change you.

"Give me ten thousand dollars," I pled with donors. "I'll take an unsuspecting Duke undergrad to Honduras, and Jesus will render her forever unfit for investment banking."

My last commencement weekend I told a graduating senior, "Look forward to meeting your mother."

"That won't happen," she said. "Mom holds you responsible for what happened to me in Haiti. She's hacked off."

"Me?"

"Mom likes the pre-Haiti me better than the me you brought back to Duke from the mission trip," she explained.

Jesus.

I brashly believe that my best teaching has arisen out of my vocation to preach. At Birmingham-Southern College (BSC) I proposed teaching a course named "Jesus, Most Interesting Person in the World," which I had polished with Duke undergrads. The BSC curriculum committee rejected the course, nervous that I might use it to "proselytize."

"I'm a Methodist! It's been so long since we have converted anybody we've forgotten how." I retitled the course "Jesus through the Centuries," unloading it on the narrow-minded liberal committee as a class on how people had viewed Jesus during different epochs.

First day of class I shut the door and whispered, "Don't tell the Religion/Philosophy Department, but this is not a history class. You want history? Go study George Washington. Jesus is worth your time only because some people believe he's here, now, messing with us even as we try to study him. But don't tell the curriculum committee! They think the Easter women were lying."

*   *   *

I've enjoyed a reputation as a friendly mentor to budding preachers and theologians. A couple of dozen protégés say that before they lurch to the left or right in their vocational odyssey, they ask, "WWWD?" I'm Mentor to their Telemachus as they benefit from my wisdom and my mistakes. A dozen of my namesakes make their way in the world, beneficiaries of that overbearing teacher who, so long ago, made me "Will."

Sometimes it's tough to have your life held up for student scrutiny. I'm up there pouring out my heart, scribbling grand truths upon the board, and they're thinking, "God, he looks old. I'm going to work out at the gym."

Students force faculty like me to render a Newmanesque *Apologia Pro Vita Sua*. I'm a better person because, in one way or another, a student barged in demanding, "How did you get here? How did you know that you were called?" coaxing me to defend vocation's choice of me.

One student baited me into admitting that I had received a number of honorary degrees. "When John McCain and I got our degrees at Colgate, the campus newspaper published our photo with the caption, 'Switched at birth? You make the call.' Maya Angelou and I were hooded at Lafayette, though only Maya got to speak."

"Thirteen!" he exclaimed. "That's almost as many as Mr. Rogers! You and Mr. Rogers snagged dozens of honorary degrees— *for the same reason!*"

Students.

I conned a Duke fraternity into letting me lead a Bible study on the Gospel of Mark. If the horde wouldn't come to my sermons, I'd take my sermons to them.

In the middle of the second session, I launched into a harangue about character and college. It was during Bill Clinton's escapades in the Oval Office, so I was off to the races.

"Young men," I lectured, "what sort of man will you grow up to be? Consider President Clinton. He has damaged his future, his family, all for sex. How many of you have had sex? Can you see jettisoning everything you believe in for that? Can you—"

A pledge's hand went up. "Like, I wonder if maybe he gets more out of it than I."

"Intriguing thought," I responded. "Let's write Bill and say, 'Bill, buddy, we've had sex, and while we enjoyed it, we wonder if you get more out of it than we. Could you explain to us . . .'"

As I said, I was on a roll. Then another student said, "Dean Willimon, would you say that your generation has a problem with sex?"

"What? No, I wouldn't say that!"

"But you and Bill Clinton are the same age. You sound like him when you talk."

"I'll have you know mine is fine South Carolina patois, not Arkansas twang!" I said. "Look, kid, I came here tonight to beat up on you, not to have my generation mocked and derided by your generation. When you write Bill, tell him that his behavior has made my moralizing diatribes much more difficult."

Students.

∗   ∗   ∗

Jesus said there's no way to achieve the friendship required for discipleship without truthful confrontation. In Matthew 18:15–17, one of the few passages in the New Testament that "church" (*ekklēsia*) is used, twice, Jesus commands, "If another member of the church sins against you, go, point out the fault. If the member listens, you have regained that one. But if you are not listened to, take one or two along with you. . . . If the member refuses to listen to them, tell it to the church, and if they don't listen to the whole church, treat 'em as no better than a gentile" (my paraphrase).

Jesus's directives seem extreme for most church squabbles. I've found that when someone offends, if I count to ten and seethe for a year or two, I usually get over it. If, on the other hand, I offend them and they refuse to suppress their anger at me, I dismiss them as touchy, overly sensitive.

I would like you to think that I'm such a nice person that I would never obey Jesus and confront you. Truth is, Jesus has a considerably higher view of friendship than that practiced in most churches, which amounts to: I promise never to hold you accountable if you'll do the same for me. Church as a gentile conspiracy of niceness, as a civil compatibility club rather than a community of truth.

A complainer charged that my classroom demeanor and my offhand comments were unprofessional. I urged him to chill out and to take courses from less demanding faculty. He sent a letter to Dean Langford in which he appealed for aid in helping me to become a better teacher.

Students.

The dean summoned us. We talked, looked over my syllabus. My eyes gradually opened to the truth of the student's concerns. I promised prayerfully to evaluate the course and make adjustments.

After the student left, the dean said, "I'm proud of the way you listened and responded."

"I can't imagine talking that way to a professor when I was a seminarian," said I.

"Nor can I," agreed Dean Langford. "Humiliating."

Humiliating?

Tom clarified: "Humbling for a student to have greater expectations for Duke Divinity School than you or I."

Students.

My last Sunday at Duke Chapel was wonderful. A huge choir and full orchestra, standing room only, people offering up small babies to be blessed on my way to be a 'Bama bishop. I preached on Eutychus (Acts 20:7–12) and bragged about all the Duke students Jesus and I had raised from the dead.

"Ichabod! The glory has fled the chapel!" (1 Sam. 4:21—see friend Stephen Chapman's 1 Samuel commentary), all wailed at the close of the service, or at least that's how I remember it.

As the bereft departed, a student came up to me and said, "I'm pissed at you. What am I to do for spiritual direction?"

I told him that I was sure that some good pastor would follow me, not to worry.

"Say, will you do much preaching where you are going?" he asked.

"As bishop I'll be preaching in at least one church every Sunday," I replied.

"Good. Maybe now you will have time to work on your organization," he said.

"What's wrong with my organization?"

"Before I came to Duke, I heard that your sermons were hard to follow because your brain just didn't work in an orderly way," he explained.

"Who said that about my preaching?"

"Like, *everybody*," he said, in love.

"Kid, are you open to a move to Alabama?" I asked. "I've been given a job where I fear that nobody will ever tell me the truth. If you dropped out of Duke and went with me to 'Bama, I could be a better preacher."

Students.

A historic responsibility of bishops is guarding the faith by teaching. I finagled dozens of opportunities to conduct workshops and lectures in my conference.

Yet, often as bishop, just as at Duke Divinity, the teacher became the taught.

"When you visit us to preach," said the rural pastor, "would you baptize a kid in our congregation?"

"Love to."

"I've been instructing him in the faith for the last few months. It will mean so much to have the bishop baptize him. By the way, he wants to be baptized by immersion." Click.

What? I believe *in baptism by total immersion, but like many of my beliefs*, I've never done it.

Patsy and I arrived at the church, a weathered clapboard building in the middle of an Alabama cornfield. Sure enough, the pastor stood on the steps with a small boy of eleven or twelve.

"Jason, it's an honor to baptize you today," I greeted him.

"They tell me you've never done one of these. I'd feel better if we rehearsed," he said.

"That's just what I was about to suggest," said I.

We went into the adjacent fellowship hall. A font, borrowed from the Baptists, was surrounded with potted plants. Jason and I walked through the ritual.

"I want to be dipped three times," he said.

"Wonderful. John Wesley was big on triple immersion, though he couldn't get many mothers to let him triple-dunk babies," I chortled nervously.

We had quite a service in the little church. I preached on baptism and then, behind the cross, everyone processed to the fellowship hall singing "Amazing Grace."

The congregation gathered around the font. After a few sentences from the Service of Baptism, I asked, "Jason, anything you would like to say to the congregation?"

"Yeah, I want to thank you, especially if you put up with me in Sunday school when I was a kid. I wouldn't have known Jesus, if you hadn't told me," Jason said. "When my mama and daddy got divorced, I thought my life had ended. But then I figured out that you were the family God wanted for me. I'm going to make you proud. I'll show you how good you are at making a disciple. You'll see."

I melted.

"Can you pull yourself together?" Jason asked.

"Y'all sing another verse of 'Amazing Grace,'" I pled.

They sang. Jason took off his shoes. I led him by the hand into the baptismal waters. God did the rest.

Church, I love you.

Late one afternoon, Lent, 1975, after finally finishing my sermon, I locked up Trinity United Methodist and made my way across the churchyard to our tiny parsonage for supper. Across the yard I saw William looking out from the parsonage window, bouncing on the back of the sofa, waiting for me.

My heart sank when I turned and saw a young man, late twenties, perhaps early thirties, coming down the church walk. *Just my rotten luck.* These drifters passed through North Myrtle Beach. Their hard luck stories differed, but all had the same ending, "Give me twenty-five dollars."

I'll head him off, give him a twenty, and be rid of him. Don't have it in me, this late in the day, to hear any more trumped-up tales of woe.

"Hello!" he called to me cheerfully.

"Hello."

"You're working late this afternoon, aren't you?"

"What can I do for you?"

"Not a thing, other than what you are already doing," he said. "Good work."

Odd comment.

"I just stopped by to tell you I think you are doing a great job here at Trinity."

"Is it Miami or Charleston that you need money to get to?" I asked with annoyance.

"Money? No," he laughed. "I just stopped by to tell you that I appreciate all you do to get the good news out to folks. Nice work. Your sermons rock."

I looked at him more carefully. He had a dark tan and was wearing khakis, scuffed loafers, and a green golf shirt. Izod. He didn't look crazy, though in this town, it can be hard to tell. I saw no hint of a weapon.

"Say," he continued, "do you get much time to read the Bible?"

"Er, uh, sure. I read Scripture every day," I answered.

So this is his shtick. He's going to wear me down with chitchat before making the ask.

"What do you think of it?" he asked.

"Uh, the Bible? I like it. I think it's good," I said.

"Thanks! 'Course, I had some great folks working with me. Glad to see it's still in print! Right?" he said jovially, buddy-tapping me lightly on the arm.

"Right," I said, my throat tightening. I assessed him closely. He looked like he had just walked off the Gator Hole Golf Course.

"Let me guess what your favorite gospel is. Luke! Am I right? I bet you like Luke as a writer, don't you?" he said. "What a cool job Luke did on the parables. Right?"

As if the busted fall stewardship campaign was not humiliating enough, now this.

"Hey, just wanted to stop by and thank you. I'm sure it's not easy in this town. Really appreciate your hard work. You're a go-getter. Pay no mind to the trustees. I'll bring 'em around, eventually. The jail ministry you guys started last year is going just great," he said, moving toward me as if to threaten a hug. "Don't worry about the stewardship thing. The money will come, I'm sure," he said patronizingly.

I took a step back. "Sorry, I didn't get your name."

"Oh, that's funny," he said, laughing. "Just Jesus to you, of course."

"Look, are you trying to be cute?" I asked.

"You think that's cute?" he responded, looking hurt. "Hey, don't want to keep you from the valuable work you are doing. But please, don't overdo it. Remember, Trinity is my problem, not yours. Help people, go ahead and preach, write, just be sure you have a good time."

"Uh, if you're Jesus, where are you headed?" I asked.

"Akron, Ohio," he said casually.

"Akron, Ohio?" I asked.

"Business," he responded.

He took my hand, drawing me uncomfortably close, giving off a slight whiff of garlic and cigarettes and said, "Well done, friend."

I received his embrace as stiffly as if I were Richard Nixon being hugged by Sammy Davis Jr. Yet as I watched him head toward the highway, I thanked God for my credulous childhood, for gates that opened and for voices that spoke in the haunted woods off Fork Shoals Road, and also for some proficiency in dealing with the comings and goings of a God both friendly and mischievous. He bounded toward Highway 17 North, where he gave me a wave, then hitched a ride from a green Toyota, and vanished toward the sunset.

That evening at supper, I related my epiphany to Patsy, just as I have told it to you. She chided me for wasting time cajoling a sadly deluded young man. I defended my actions. When one works a while with Jesus, one chastens one's notions of delusional.

Later that night, Patsy stood in our miniature bedroom, thoughtfully holding her toothbrush, and said, "One thing still bothers me. Why Akron, Ohio?"

What a Jesus we have as friend.

9

Unforeseen Commission

Others mocking said, These men are full of new wine. But
Peter, standing up with the eleven, lifted up his voice, and
said unto them, Ye men of Judaea, . . . hearken to my words:
For these are not drunken, as ye suppose, seeing it is but
the third hour of the day. But this is that which was spoken
by the prophet Joel; And it shall come to pass in the last
days, saith God, I will pour out of my Spirit upon all flesh:
and your sons and your daughters shall prophesy, and your
young men shall see visions, and your old men shall dream
dreams: And on my servants and on my handmaidens I will
pour out in those days of my Spirit; and they shall prophesy:
And I will shew wonders in heaven above, and signs in the
earth beneath; blood, and fire, and vapour of smoke. . . .
And it shall come to pass, that whosoever shall call on the
name of the Lord shall be saved. (Acts 2:13–21)

As Pentecostal smoke settles, a scoffing street mob sneers, "It's
like Jesus was still with 'em; they're drunk!" In the face of the

mob, Peter preaches. *Peter?* Remember where we left Peter, in the courtyard with the maid while our Lord was being tortured?

"You were with the Galilean," she charged.

And Peter, the alleged "Rock," said, "I never really knew him."

Now, with the descent of the Spirit, Peter accidentally preaches. Joel preached that whereas just a few Hebrew prophets got to speak up for God, there would be a great comedic new age when everyone—old and young, maids, janitors, men and women—would be accidental preachers.

Peter's sermon (incredibly short, devoid of illustrations, culturally irrelevant, yet astoundingly effective) gives evidence that the Spirit-induced new age is today. Now anybody God chooses, even betrayers like Peter or me, can be enlisted for prophecy.

Methodism practices a "sent ministry." No congregation can hire a Methodist pastor; preachers are sent by the bishop. Being a Methodist preacher is un-American: subordinating family, personal goals, and sometimes happiness to the mission of Jesus Christ as interpreted by people like Legrand Moody, Billy Graham, Betty Achtemeier, Carlyle Marney, or a kid named Jason.

In a culture of presumptively free, self-made people, it's a reach to believe that I am accidentally determined, that the life I'm living isn't my own. Throughout my ministry I've had to be re-called, learning again not to resent being re-sent. My worth is in the message with which I have been entrusted, a message more meaningful than the messenger.

*   *   *

Methodist political junkies predicted there was no way in God's name the six hundred members of the 2004 Southeastern Jurisdictional Conference would elect me as bishop.

No campus minister had been elected bishop.

I had been absent from my home conference, South Carolina, for twenty years.

I had allowed Duke Chapel to be used for same-sex unions.

I had never led a prestigious Methodist church.

My negative paper trail was miles long.

Some were still sore about my *Christian Century* article "My Dog the Methodist," a spoof of UMC evangelism fiascoes.

I had ridiculed the alleged evangelicals of the Confessing Movement as having nothing to confess but "I believe in straight sex."

Few bishops forgave me for calling the Council of Bishops "the bland leading the bland."

"Will, if you didn't have such a smart mouth," said Bishop Bev Jones, "you could be a bishop. It's a pity." This from one of the three bishops who actually supported me.

I was the second bishop elected.

"I told you it was a bad idea to invite the Holy Spirit to barge into this meeting," groused one of my opponents to his buddies. "Now pray to God that Willimon won't be assigned to Kentucky."

Fifty ballots later, when the voting was over, it was very late on Friday evening. We new bishops were hurriedly assembled behind the stage, and the chair of the Episcopacy Committee said, "Give me your phone numbers. Go home. I'll call you sometime tonight and tell you where you are being sent."

He added, "Don't ever treat your pastors this way."

At 2:40 in the morning the phone rings. A south Georgia drawl asks, "Guess where you're going? Birmingham." *Damn.*

"Patsy is as thrilled as I. Which of my talents suggested me for Birmingham?" I asked.

"Somebody's got to go there."

Here I am, Lord, I have heard you calling at 2:40 a.m.

The worst day of being bishop was the next—Saturday's orientation by the senior bishops. We baby bishops were consigned to a windowless room at Lake Junaluska where for five hours we were pounded with advice: *Don't give your cell phone number to anybody. Handshakes are more appropriate for the office of bishop than hugs. Don't let people call you by your first name. You are to be the last person in every processional. Take care eating fish at church dinners. Never become friends with the clergy you must oversee. Always have a bottle of hand sanitizer with you at church receptions.*

The nadir was the pinning ceremony, where a senior bishop tacked the red episcopal lapel pin on each new bishop.

If the bishops had asked for a ceremonial consult with Boy Scout Troop Nine or even Nu Chapter of Pi Kappa Alpha, the pinning ceremony might have worked.

I never wore the pin. Nor did I order the "real twenty-four-carat gold episcopal ring." Though I didn't know much about the United Methodist episcopacy, I knew that if I required a cheap lapel pin to shore up my authority, I was in trouble. I wish that Jesus had authorized lapel pins, Boy Scout badges, corporal's stripes, judge's wigs, Tasers, or doctoral hoods to give God's servants clout, but that's not how Jesus works.

If you don't believe me, you are welcomed to inspect my official UMC episcopal lapel pin where it rests, unused, in Patsy's jewelry box in the top left drawer of our bedroom dresser.

*　　*　　*

At age ten, I was doing time in Miss McDaniel's sixth grade class, dutifully copying inanities off the blackboard, when I got the call. A note was delivered by one of the toadies from the front office. Old Lady McDaniel read the note and then called out, "Willimon. Mr. Harrelson" (the intimidating, iron-fisted, ancient principal) "wants to see you."

With trepidation, I lifted my desktop, put away my things, and trudged toward the principal's office. Passing an open door, I saw a classmate look out with pity, praying, *Thank God it's him and not me.* Ascending the gallows, I went over in my mind all the possible misunderstandings that could have led to this portentous subpoena. *I was only a distant witness to the rock-through-the-gym-window incident, in no way a perpetrator or even passive conspirator.*

"Listen carefully. I do not intend to repeat myself," said the principal, looking down at me. "You, go down Tindal two blocks and turn left, go two more blocks, number 15. I've got a message to be delivered. You tell Jimmy Spain's mother if he's not in school by this afternoon, I'm reporting her for truancy."

So this wasn't about me. It was worse. *God help me. Jimmy Spain, toughest thug of all the sixth grade.* If we lived in a just world, Jimmy should have been in the eighth. *And what in God's name is "truancy"?*

Somber thoughts tormented me as I journeyed down Tindal, bidding farewell to the safety of the schoolyard, turned left, walked two more blocks, marveling that the world actually went about its business while we did time in school.

Under a darkening sky, the last two blocks descended into a not-nice part of town unknown to me or any of my friends, a sad neighborhood that hid behind the school. Number 15 was a small house, peeling paint, bare yard—just the sort of house you'd expect Jimmy Spain to be holed up in, rough, sinister. A reassuring blue Buick was parked in front. As I fearfully approached the walk, a man emerged, letting the screen door slam as he stepped off the porch, adjusted his tie, stretched his suspenders, and lit a cigar.

"Are you, Mr. . . . Spain, sir?" As the words came out of my mouth, I remembered that everybody at school said that Jimmy was so mean because he didn't have a daddy.

The man looked down at me, pulled taut his tie, and guffawed. "Mr. Spain?" Haw, haw, haw. "Mr. Spain, my ass."

He sent up a cloud of smoke, pushed himself into his Buick, and sped off. (Not until the eighth grade did someone whisper the word for what Jimmy's mother did for a living. At the Boy Scout Court of Honor I saw again the man who had brushed me aside. A member of city council, he pinned on my First Class Scout badge.)

I stepped on the rotten porch and tapped the soiled screen door. My heart sank. The door was opened by none other than Jimmy Spain. His reptilian green eyes enlarged when he saw me, startled as much by me as I was by him. Before Jimmy could say anything, the door was pulled back and a woman in a faded blue terrycloth bathrobe inspected me, looking over Jimmy's shoulder.

"What do you want?" she asked. A mother smoking, and in a bathrobe, even though it's midday?

"Er, I'm from the school. The principal sent me, to, uh . . ."

"Principal! What does that old fool want?"

"Er, he sent me to say that we, er, that is, that everybody at school, that we all miss Jimmy and wish he were there today."

"What?" she sneered, pulling Jimmy toward her.

"It's like a special day and everyone wants Jimmy there. We are doing some special stuff. Music maybe. Ice cream, for all I know. Everybody thinks it won't be as special if Jimmy's not there. At least, I think that's what he said."

Jimmy—the thug who could beat up any kid at Donaldson Elementary, even ninth graders, anytime he wanted—Jimmy peered out at me in . . . wonderment. Suddenly this hood, feared by all, looked small, being clutched by his mother, his eyes embarrassed, hanging on my every stammering word.

"You tell that old man it's none of his damn business what I do with James. James," she said, looking down at him (*"James"?*), "you want to go to that stupid school today or not?"

Jimmy didn't take his eyes off me as he wordlessly nodded assent.

"Suit yourself. Get your stuff. And take that dollar off the dresser to buy lunch. I ain't got nothing here."

In a flash he was away and back. His mother stood at the door and stared suspiciously, and after giving Jimmy an unimaginable peck on the cheek, watched as we walked off the rotting porch, down the walk, and back toward Tindal Avenue. We said not a word. I had previously lacked the courage to speak to Jimmy the Hood, and Jimmy the Tough had never had any reason, thank the Lord, to speak to me. Walking back to school that afternoon was no time to begin.

I think we didn't talk because each of us knew, without knowing, that we had been part of something bigger than us, more than words could say.

We walked up the steps to the school, took a right, and wordlessly turned toward the principal's office. Jimmy allowed himself to be led by me. I handed him off to the principal's secretary. For the first time Jimmy seemed not mean and threatening, but small. As the secretary led him away, Jimmy turned and looked back with a look of . . . I don't know, maybe regret, embarrassment? But it could have also been thanks, gratitude.

That evening, when I narrated my day to my mother at supper of minute steak and mashed potatoes, she exclaimed, "That is the most outrageous thing I've ever heard! Sending a young child out in the middle of the school day to fetch a truant. And on that street! Mr. Harrelson ought to have his head examined. Don't you ever allow anyone again to put you in that position. Sending a child!"

My mother was wrong. That day was my best at Donaldson Elementary. That day explained everything, preparation for the rest of my accidental life, my first comedic brush with a God who thinks nothing of commandeering ordinary boys and handing them outrageous assignments.

I didn't know then, but that day, on Tindal Avenue, old man Harrelson became an agent of prevenient grace, preparing me for the accidental life that was not my own, dress rehearsal for the comedy that commenced on a midsummer night two decades later when I knelt before a bishop who laid on hands

and said, "You, go down Tindal two blocks and turn left, go
to seminary and grad school, go obediently to the churches I
send you, be a bishop, write and talk. God has a message to
be delivered."

Afterword

KATE BOWLER

This book is a lie. There is absolutely nothing accidental about Will Willimon.

When Will first declared that he was writing his memoirs, I was thrilled. Thank God, this man will achieve a measure of self-understanding, I told him. But when I finally read the pages of this book, I called him to my office and asked him plainly why he had not written about his most defining feature.

"I have a defining feature?" he asked, grandly. (We might add the adverb "grandly" after every sentence ever concluded by Bishop Will Willimon of South Carolina. The man is nothing if not grand.)

"Yes," I persisted. "You never mention that you are undoubtedly the most impatient man who ever entered the ministry. It's as if you strode into the pulpit on your first day and said, 'We are going to need to move things along now.' You write books faster than most people can think. And you are deeply intolerant of mediocrity."

And then Bishop Will Willimon of South Carolina gave a bit of a harrumph and returned to his office. Grandly.

Less than twenty-four hours later I received an email from him with no preamble and only a single link to a website. I clicked on it to discover a video of Will, standing comfortably at a podium, prepared to deliver a sermon. "Our Lord and Savior, Jesus Christ, was often chided for something that would come to define his ministry: *a holy impatience.*" And then he looked directly into the camera with a languid pause.

The sermon that followed is precisely why Will Willimon became the kind of preacher and man he is. Anything that sparks his imagination must immediately, with no dallying, be transformed into something useful for the church. It is the reason he has written over eighty books and thousands upon thousands of sermons. It is why he has opened his home and his office to more clergy, parishioners, and students than I have met in my lifetime. He moves at a pace of life that is inconceivable for most with his loud and irresistible humor that clears the way before him. He is his own John the Baptist.

This memoir is about the comedy of calling and the absurdity of being chosen by a God whose purposes simultaneously elevate and level us. We devote ourselves to the grand cause of joining God in bringing heaven to earth, but mostly we find ourselves doing paperwork and trying to find better parking. We want to *feel* called, but we are asked to simply act like it.

In a very personal way, I have learned the benefits of meeting someone like Will, who insisted on acting like he was called. Called to sit with my parents in their shock and grief over my sudden cancer diagnosis. Called to be at the hospital at 4 a.m. in those awful moments before a surgery. Called to check in and ask me how I am, only to make fun of me because it is what I prefer. A called person is a person who insists on being a witness to the presence of the Holy Spirit in classrooms and hospital rooms, wherever that may be. And in this case, it involved the flagrant abuse of hospital visiting hours by taking the clerical collar out of his glove box, or wherever he stores it, to show up when the kingdom of God did not feel near enough.

This book is an invitation to experience wonderment at the vagaries and beauty of being called. And a reminder of the sense of adventure that a life with God should be. We ought to live in such a way that we are both expectant of and bewildered by the miracles concocted from our lives—our hopes, quirks, and gifts. When the ministry of Will Willimon is finally at an end, I fully expect that God will look down from the clouds and declare grandly that this was a man in a great hurry to live entirely on purpose.

Index

Index

Hitler, Adolf, 133, 182–83
Holmer, Paul, 157–60
Homer, 58, 205
Hooker, Richard, 174
Hopkins, Gerard Manley, 162
Hughes, Langston, 103
Humbert, Humbert, 161–62
Hume, David, 158, 169
Hunsinger, George, 167
Hunt, James, 101
Hunter, Rodney, 81–82
Hurlbut, Jesse Lyman, 19–20
Hursey, Peggy, 84, 194

Isaiah, 51–53

James, 8
James, William, 57–58
Jason, 217–18, 224
Jefferson, Thomas, 94
Jeremiah, 95, 105, 117, 121, 182
Jesus, 6–9, 11, 19, 27–29, 32–33,
    35, 39, 54–55, 57–58, 63, 66, 69,
    72, 77–83, 88, 91–93, 95, 97–98,
    101, 104, 106–8, 111–14, 119–20,
    123–25, 128, 130, 133–34, 136,
    141–43, 145–47, 149, 151, 154–55,
    159, 161, 166, 168, 170–73,
    176, 181–82, 185, 187–89, 192,
    195–96, 206, 210–11, 213–14,
    217, 220–21, 223, 226, 227,
    234
Joe, 200–201
Johnson, Lady Bird, 143
Johnson, Lyndon, 143
Johnson, Magic, 88
Johnson, Samuel, 28
Jones, Bevel, 208, 225
Jones, Tom, 37
Jones, Tuck, 208
Joplin, Janis, 120
José, 114
Joseph, 32, 98, 146

Kant, Immanuel, 158
Keller, Helen, 141
Kennedy, Teddy, 127
Keohane, Nan, 119, 125
Kierkegaard, Søren, 10, 35, 52,
    158–60, 172, 198
King, Coretta Scott, 87
King, Larry, 88
King, Martin Luther, Jr., 69–70,
    116
Koppel, Ted, 119
Krzyzewski, Mike, 120
Kuyper, Abraham, 204

Langford, Thomas L., 129, 167, 214
Lawrence, D. H., 109
Lee, Harper, 168
Lee, Robert E., 94
Levertov, Denise, 162
Lewis, C. S., 2, 22–23
Lischer, Richard, 119, 182, 209
Logan, Frank, 156–57
Louis XIV, 182
Luther, Martin, 170
Lynn, Hawley, 182

Mann, Thomas, 154, 161
Mark, 151
Marney, Carlyle, 46–48, 58, 66,
    68–70, 103, 126, 175, 185, 208–9,
    224
Mary (mother of Jesus), 32, 55, 63,
    95, 98
Mary Grace, 178–79
Massillon, Jean-Baptiste, 182
McCain, John, 212
McCormack, Bruce, 167
McCullers, Carson, 62
McDaniel, Miss, 227
Mead, Margaret, 81
Meadors, Jack, 193
Mencken, H. L., 66
Miller, Stephen, 115

239